Dedication

To: *The Friday Priest Prayer Group*
Brother Pancratius Boudreau, C. SS.R
and
Sister Alice Price R.S.M.

Table of Contents

The Power of David's Key

Monsignor Vincent M. Walsh

Key of David Publications
204 Haverford Road
Wynnewood, PA 19096

Ecclesiastical Approval

    This book has been submitted to the Archdiocisan Censor Librorum who has stated in writing that there is nothing in this book that is contrary to faith or morals.

    According to the new canonical norms a NIHIL OBSTAT or IMPRIMATUR are no longer used for this category of printed materials.

Cover and Text design: Sr. Maryanne Johnston

Table of Contents

Prologue

Title, Dream and Vision

". . . I am the Root and Offspring of David,
   the Morning Star shining bright"
                        (Rev. 22:16)

He said to them, "Then how is it that David
under the Spirit's influence calls him 'lord' as
he does:
   'The Lord said to my lord, Sit at my right hand,
   until I humble your enemies beneath your feet'.
                        (Matt. 22:43-44 — cf: Mk 12:36
                                    and Luke 20:42)

"To the presiding spirit of the Church of Phila-
delphia, write this:
   "The holy one, the true,
   who wields David's Key. ."   (Rev. 3:7)

For many years, I tried to write a book about religious experiences. However, the varied jottings never fell into place until one night in prayer, God gave me the title to this book, "The Power of David's Key". With that, everything began.

There was the scriptural claim of Jesus that the messiah had been called "Lord" by David. Psalm 110 which says those words, "The Lord said to my Lord: Sit at my right hand till I make your enemies your footstool", also contains that sentence special to every priest "You are a priest forever, according to the order of Melchizedeck". The Davidic anointing and priesthood go together.

The following explains the title, the dream and the vision.

1. David and Saul

David stands in contrast to Saul. Saul held an external office bestowed by God but with no personal relationship to God. David's anointing, however, was two-fold, the external office of king and the internal anointing of personal friendship with God.

"Then, Samuel, with the horn of oil annointed him in the midst of his brothers; and from that day on, the spirit of the Lord rushed upon David."(1 Sam 6:13)

In Jesus, there were also two workings of the Spirit. The first was the mystery of the Incarnation. The second was the human yielding to the Spirit that led even to the cross.

Every priest is given the external anointing of office, bestowing on him the Church's powers. What the priest must bring is his human yielding to the Spirit. He needs the full power of David's Key.

2. "Go To My Priests"

In October 1972, after a tremendous year and a half of a charismatic ministry to laity and sisters, the Lord spoke and told me to go to his priests.

This was the last thing in the world I wanted to hear. To socialize with priests, or to work with priests was fine. But to pray with priests or to try to teach priests, was just not for me. But the word was clear, so I began.

A few interested priests were gathered, and were asked for a committal to pray together. The group was small and committal was for Saturday morning at various rectories. The number who actually gathered was from 2 to 5, but always somebody was there.

Since most who came were involved in diocesan work, we began to meet on Fridays after office hours. In March 1973, the group decided to be available to every priest, so the location was moved, and the time changed to Thursday, an evening that seemed appropriate to priesthood. Ever since then the group has met faithfully. Currently 20 to 25 are involved and 8 to 12 are present each week. Many other priests have been with us. A number of priests who had left the active ministry have used the group as a stepping stone back.

More important the group has been the core for other outreaches to priests through the monthly priest prayer dinners and the annual priests' conference which in 1980 attracted 135 priests.

Four years ago, I was asked to begin at the seminary. Since then a seminary prayer group has flourished. Recently requests have come for priest retreats. So Philadelphia priests now go forth to various parts of the country.

The most important gift, however, is a new level of priest relationship, especially priests praying with one another.

All of this is written so you will know that the following pages are not just theory, but the Davidic anointing is happening in Philadelphia and is meant to happen all over the world.

In the name of the priests in the Church of Philadelphia, I say to you,

What we have seen and heard we proclaim to you
so that you may share life with us.   (1 Jn 1:3)

3. The Dream

So, the work with priests has flourished, but the dream is only beginning. Religious experiences are not yet part of mainstream Catholicism, and for most Catholics the religious experience gift remains unopened.

My dream is:

1) That every priest would receive the gift of religious experience.
2) That he would learn how to release the gift in all of his parishioners.
3) That no one could attend his parish liturgy and not experience God.
4) That the common gift of religious experiences would form parish community, and the parishioners would see themselves as brothers and sisters through common Baptism.

Currently, the Church believes it can sanctify by sacraments, clear teaching, good organization and institutions. It doesn't see fully the importance of religious experiences. Yet, without religious experiences, we priests are not faithful to the power of David's Key.

4. The Vision

The "vision" for this book occurred in June 1975 during our priest's Charismatic Retreat.

A group of us had been moving quickly into extraordinary powers of God. I saw that God wanted us to go slowly, to wait for all of his priests to "catch up", so to speak. It was far more important for all priests to be awakened to the spirit, even in a beginning fashion than for a few of us to move so quickly ahead that no one could even see or grasp what was happening.

Ever since that date, I have felt God's call to try to explain in simple language, understood by every priest, the whole world of the inner movements of God called religious experiences.

Then every priest, having both the external powers of his office and the internal relationship to God, would wield the power of David's Key.

Part One

The Personal Religious Experience

Two religious experiences, seventeen years apart, are landmarks in my life.

In the summer of 1954, I was an eighteen year old, just home from my first seminary year, deeply influenced by "A Seminarian at His Predieu", and seeking to be the "priest of prayer", the author Fr. Nash, S.J. so stressed.

Each morning, an hour before mass, I rose from sleep to attempt to pray. After about two weeks of this effort, around the feast of the Sacred Heart, the gift of prayer was given. It was bestowed through God's touches on my imagination, and was completed by a personal knowledge of Jesus Christ in whose presence I would walk from then on.

During that summer, the initial gift deepened, was strengthened by the return to the seminary and was completed by a prayer experience on Thanksgiving morning, 1954, when there was the realization of the presence of the indwelling of Jesus.

These religious experiences led to a conversion, not from a seriously disordered life, but from a selfish to an unselfish life and to a forgiving attitude.

A year later, the experiences led to a summer apostolate among the immigrant Puerto Ricans. The prayer gifts kept alive zeal and the desire for priesthood, made the road to ordination in 1962 a much smoother one, and provided the impulse for parish work.

The second religious experience was associated with Charismatic Renewal, and occurred the evening of May 1, 1971, two weeks after beginning a committed involvement in a local prayer group. That experience involved yielding to prayer tongues, and has been the door to my ministry since that time. The two gifts — of prayer and prayer tongues are the foundation of every day of my priesthood.

The following three chapters are written because I believe those two gifts are rooted in Baptism, and are the basic personal religious experiences for everyone.

1

The Beginning Gift

Suddenly looking around they no longer saw anyone with them – only Jesus. (Mk. 9:8)

. . . On the Lord's day I was caught up in ecstacy and I heard behind me a piercing voice...

(Rev. 1:10)

"Who are you, sir?" he asked. The voice answered "I am Jesus, the one you are persecuting. Get up and go into the city, where you will be told what to do." (Acts 11:5-6)

Religious experiences begin in the strangest places. For the last 10 years, I have heard hundreds of stories of beginning religious experiences.

These stories, and my own study, have convinced me of one thing — there is a definite, beginning religious experience.

The gift is available to everyone — the first adult fruits of Baptism.

This beginning involves Jesus, and the person seeking Him. It involves changes — new hope, new trust, God's light overcoming darkness. The person literally experiences the promise of John (C7:37).

". . . From within him rivers of living water shall flow . . ."

The gift is personal, bestowed at a moment chosen by God. No way exists to define that beginning. So, I can only tell the stories, trusting that one of these will ignite the gift.

1. Seeing How Another Received The Gift

In August 1962, I attended the Newman Club Convention in Pittsburgh. During that week, a group of priests were at supper and the discussion turned to the Cursillo Movement. One priest said that there were two great events in his life — his ordination and his Cursillo weekend.

Never having made a Cursillo, I didn't understand that statement. Only later, when I heard people describe what happened to them on their Cursillo, did I realize that my 1954 prayer experience was the same as the other priest's Cursillo gift.

Both of our prayer gifts were a beginning, just as ordination is. Ordination introduces the priest to an external Church ministry. The prayer gift should initiate a life of religious experiences. Without these religious experiences, we priests are just Sauls and not Davids.

2. Tears In Chapel

I had known this priest well. In time, he came to the prayer group and shared as best he could, but there was no experience of Jesus. One night in chapel, he asked me to pray for him. The tears started to come and strange words of praise came from his lips. He had received the gift.

Since then, much has happened. On the surface, he is still the same, but his faith, his work, his prayer, his priesthood are all changed.

During these years, he has done some things of permanent value for the Archdiocese, mostly because he took every decision to prayer instead of acting on impulse. Many who will receive the benefits of his work, won't even realize the changes that began that night in chapel.

3. The People Gave The Gift

It was 1972, and we were running a retreat weekend. Suddenly this priest showed up, walking with a group of people. They had led him into their group, and by their love of him into the initial experience of Jesus.

Later the priest was told he had cancer — a very severe form with many questions of whether he would live. There were many trips to the hospital. One stands out. It was Christmas time and besides the cancer, there was hepatitis. As I walked into his room, unaware of the gowns at the door, he said, "You better check, because I'm infectious." I checked, put on the gown and spent a Christmas visit.

There was no sadness. In the middle of everything there was joy and a quiet "I know I am going to get better," Slowly, he has gotten better, very much better, with no signs of the cancer, and an ability to return to full, active ministry.

His people had not only loved him, they had led him to Jesus, a gift he needed when little natural hope was present.

4. The People Led Him, Too

He was searching and questioning — not about Jesus but about priesthood, and each attempt to revive a vocation was a failure. Not knowing any of these difficulties, former parishioners told him about the gift of religious experience and prevailed on him to come with them.

He came and the gift was planted — a gift which has grown ever since.

Later he helped a long time priest friend to find stability. That friend once remarked to me, "I've known him since grade school, and this is not the same person. He has talents and gifts no one ever dreamed of".

That priest speaks now with great power, but all because former parishioners wanted to share with him their new-found gift of Jesus.

5. The Business-Man Priest

He approached everything with reason. He was hard-headed, the business-man priest, who analyzed everything, but a wonderful talent.

So, when he first hear about widespread religious experiences, he approached and sought, but with reason. For a year or so, he circled the whole thing, attracted but not yielding.

One Pentecost, the Lord said to go pray with him. Since the Lord had already prepared him for a Pentecost gift, there was no awkwardness. Just the laying on of hands, and a period of extended prayer. From that day, a constant growth has occurred.

He is still the business-man priest, the one who always analyzes, but the core of his priesthood is now a God-experience.

6. Getting Through His First Meeting

He sat restless as the prayer meeting was to begin. It was his first prayer meeting and I have never seen anyone so afraid. God was thoughtful, though. This night's meeting was going to be shortened, because President Nixon was resigning at 9:00 P.M.

The next day at the office, he was all smiles — he had "gotten through" his first prayer meeting. He has been there ever since — every week of the year. He also has reached out to priests off the active ministry. He brings them in from everywhere. There have been lasting results, including the death-bed restoration of an elderly priest to good standing, complete with the full priestly burial rites.

All the good he has done, and all the support he has been, goes back to that first fearful night, as he "got through" his first prayer meeting.

7. A CYO Retreat

This priest took his CYO on a retreat, and came back with the beginning gift. The next week he sat in my office trying to explain the experience, hoping that he didn't look too silly.

His world was programs — all types of programs with great creativity. Everything that could be tried for the young, he did.

Now he realized that the young could come to know Jesus. His is yet an untapped gift, but there is time, and someday the gift of that retreat will come to full blossom.

2

Needing Religious Experiences

"... although by this time you should be teaching others, you need to have someone teach you again the basic elements of the oracles of God; you need milk, not solid food ..."   (Heb. 5:12)

During Vatican II, as change followed upon change, people asked frequently, "Do we really need that?" In other words, change is difficult and usually avoided if possible.

On the other hand, when we know we need something, we search for it until we have found it, we seek it and welcome it.

Widespread religious experiences have not been the normal state of the Catholic Church since the second century. Church history records moments of fervor or revival: "Ages of Faith" when the power of the Christendom held sway; and the beginnings of religious orders, when the founders and their immediate followers all seemed to experience God.

Yet the normal state of the Catholic Church has been the day-to-day "going about God's business", serving faithfully a God who is not experienced.

It is not a "far-away" God, because the Catholic teaching on sacraments has Him very near. It is just not a God who is personally experienced on a widespread scale.

The reasons for this state are not hard to find and seem basically rooted in the Church's longevity (2000 years) and its gigantic worldwide size. Religious experiences always seem to be for the few or for a period of time. They represent a high level of religious fidelity to the Spirit.

The following stories try to carve into the priest's heart a need for religious experiences.

1. Why No Panic?

It's Dec. 23rd. I was asked to assist at confessions this afternoon. I stayed 20 minutes for there were just very few who came.

In my first parochial years, 1962 to 1964, confessional lines were long. When I returned from Rome in the summer of 1965, a great change had occurred. The confessional lines have been going down ever since. About 1970, the Archdiocese even said that resident priests need not hear confessions, since the great need was no longer there.

The Reconciliation Sacrament, like so many other parts of Church life, is becoming a remnant of the past. Only the liturgy seems to remain well-attended. Yet the Church shows no panic, no sense of searching. The priest just goes through his usual tasks. The younger priests don't even have a memory of what used to be.

The priesthood I was ordained into is far different than today's priesthood. The Church has suffered a loss of power brought about by the modern world.

In that sense of loss, I searched and God was kind enough to show me certain elements that can restore power to the Church.

I then searched for a term so I could explain what I had found to the whole Church. The term is *"religious experiences."*

2. A Message and an Experience

A week ago, John Lennon, the ex-Beatle, was killed, prompting a world-wide outpouring of those touched by his life. He brought both a message and an experience. A couple of us priests, in the midst of the publicity, were trying to decipher just what his message was. It seemed pantheistic mixed with humanistic hope. His power certainly didn't lie in the clarity of his message. His world-wide power lay in combining his message with the experience of his music.

In His Church Jesus placed both message and experience. The message is clear, with the most beautiful theology — far beyond the dreams and hopes of man. The message begins with a loving Father, who sent His Son, who in turn gave us His living Spirit, so all history has meaning and besides that, the seeds of eternal life are placed in our mortal bodies.

But that beautiful message has power only if combined with an experience. To forsake religious experiences; to move these experiences off to the side; to say it doesn't matter if we experience the Trinity or not; is to be left with only a message.

Here in Philadelphia, as elsewhere, rock groups fill our indoor arena, and in good weather, our outdoor stadium. Some have a message — others don't — but all bring an immediate, personal and communal experience.

The Church has the same powers, but for too long they have been locked away. So the rock groups pack them in by providing a communal yet personal experience.

3. Running Out of Gas

A number of years ago, I was invited by a class of theologians to speak to them about religious experiences. It was an informal setting, so at the appointed time everyone sat down and I began. A few minutes later, some others arrived, causing everyone to shift around. This provided a break in the talk and gave me a chance to turn to the seminarian who had invited me. I asked him if I was speaking on the correct topic. His reply sort of startled me, "Yes it is, but I think I better tell you ahead of time that none of us really believes in all this." The others had heard the remark, so all I could think was "wait until you run out of gas in the priesthood, and maybe then you will be ready to 'believe in all this.'"

Long before any priest runs out of gas, he should ask himself, "What drives me?"

Often the reasons are natural — to do something with his life; to have a certain satisfaction in his work; to see something accomplished.

Without the gift of religious experiences, the priest will have problems with two sets of drives.

Work accomplishments can move a priest to activity but they cannot deliver him from the evil within himself. The work can even justify the evil.

Secondly, work drives bring their own frustrations. Who can deliver the hard-working priest from feelings that it is all in vain; or that people are not responding; or that so much is done but so little accomplished? The strain begins to show and the priest has nowhere to go and no one to set him free.

Without religious experiences, the priest's relationship to Jesus Christ is tenuous, the result of a cultural faith. What gas is he running on, and what's he going to do when it runs out?

4. *How Real Is Jesus?*

The feast of the Ascension was always puzzling to me. Just what did the feast mean?

Eventually I understood, and the Ascension began to be very important. Jesus entered into His Lordship, and because He sat at the Father's right hand, He held all history in His hands and was able to intervene.

On Ascension Day 1971, I was celebrating mass for the medical students and nurses at Jefferson Hospital. The homily that day reflected my new understanding of Jesus as Lord. After the homily, one girl got up to disagree very vehemently, saying "You have the idea that Jesus is real, that He still exists somewhere and that He enters into daily life. Well, that's not my idea of Jesus at all. For me, Jesus' power lies in the fact that He gave us a model and that he taught a nice doctrine, but I can't believe that Jesus is as real as you make him."

The two views of Jesus contrasted greatly. The homily had contained stories of Jesus intervening. That realness was too much for her.

How real is Jesus for you? The answer has little to do with theology and much to do with religious experiences. Religious experiences highlight Jesus, they bring Him into focus and into the foreground.

The purpose of religious experiences is to make the risen Jesus real for the person, just as the visions made the risen Jesus real for the disciples.

These experiences are especially important in the modern world for two reasons:

1) The multitude of other experiences can easily wipe away any vestige of religious faith.
2) The problems ahead will demand that people know that Jesus is real.

5. *The Priest Scholar*

Sometimes priests feel that their intellectual talents make religious experiences unimportant. During the theological dissent that followed Pope Paul VI's encyclical on birth control, a priest scholar stated that he didn't agree with the teaching, but that it wouldn't affect his life, because he was in the intellectual world and didn't have pastoral responsibility.

That statement highlights the problem of a priest using his task to detach himself from the rest of the Church. The more highly trained a priest is, the more skilled he is in some phases of Church life — the more he tends to excuse himself from seeking religious experiences.

The priest claims he has this new book to write; or that series of lectures to give; or this new branch of study to explore.

The work of the priest scholar, not rooted in a personal experience of Jesus Christ and not seeking God's dominion over his gifts, is of little real use to the Church, no matter how many books he has sold. The truly great minds — Augustine and Thomas — were rooted in God experiences.

Religious experiences will bring the scholar to where the people are, and he can then put his gift into simple words that the masses will understand.

6. *Holding Out Our Hands*

A few minutes ago, as I was distributing Holy Communion, a little four year old boy was at the end of the first pew and obviously interested in receiving what everybody else was getting.

After a while, he realized that the secret was to put out his hand, because then the priest would place the host there. So, for the rest of the line he patiently and quietly stood at the end of his pew with his hand out to me, much to the delight of everybody else in line. At the end I had to put my arm around him and say, "When you grow up a little, I'll be able to give this to you." He grinned and said "Oh, thanks, Father!"

The same is true in receiving religious experiences. We have to keep our hands out seeking them and when it is the correct time, the heavenly Father will gladly bestow them.

The Catholic Encyclopedia states:

"In the 4 centuries from Luther to William James there is one common note in all of Western Christianity aside from Catholicism, namely that religious experiences are the ultimate criterion and rule of faith. Every constraint of dogma, authority, and speculative reason is to give way to it." (cf. Experience, Religious - Vol. 5)

The Catholic Church has rightly refused to say that religious experiences are the salvation act. (The initiation sacraments are that.) The Church has rightly refused to claim that religious experiences are the essence of sanctity (charity is that).

But after we have accepted all the clear Catholic teaching concerning religious experiences, we are still supposed to stand in the first pew with our hand out awaiting this beginning gift from the Heavenly Father.

7. *Catching On To The Secret*

One time a religious sister showed up at our prayer meeting. Afterwards, I had a chance to speak with her and ask her how she enjoyed the evening. Her reply was, "Father, these people are wonderful, but they have too many prayer gifts for me to be part of this."

In spite of this, the sister continued to come. A few weeks later, I again had a chance to ask the same question. Her reply was different, "Father, I am catching on to the secret." I asked her what secret she discovered. She replied, "you become like these people, just by coming." She had caught on.

That's a basic Catholic teaching — that the community bestows the gifts.

All of these stories are about the initial gift of religious experiences. They stress how available the gift is. Hopefully, the priest is feeling — how can I get this gift?

Even to say — just ask, search, believe — is not concrete enough. The final word is — go find another priest (or lay person) who has experienced Jesus Christ and let him pray with you and over you. Do this on a regular basis.

Probably this is the best way of all, because you are going to need some help, advice and support to move beyond the initial experience.

3

Seeking Religious Experiences

. . . You have drawn near . . to Jesus, the media-tor of a new covenant . .   (Heb. 12:22-24)

. . . But know that the reign of God is near.
(Luke 10:11)

Oh, that today you would hear his voice.
(Ps. 95:7)

"Tomorrow and tomorrow and tomorrow" — the famous Augustinian lines describing his putting off the search for Jesus. The final discovery — "How late have I loved you". In between was the conversion experience of tears, after he heard the words "Take and read, take and read."

Each day has so many demands that seemingly have to be met. So the seeking for Jesus becomes a "tomorrow" promise.

If Jesus is sought only tomorrow, He will not be found today. These stories urge everyone to seek the Lord while He may be found.

1. *Nobody Ever Told Me To Ask*

During my seminary years, the Paulist Fathers published a monthly bulletin on convert-making. Frequently this bulletin would contain stories of converts who hadn't become Catholics years before "because nobody ever asked me."

Most priests don't seek religious experiences because "nobody ever told them to." The seminary stressed discipline, study, "making your meditation", saying your rosary, doing your spiritual reading. Somewhere in the midst of all that, there might be a religious experience or two, but that wasn't too important.

I guess that should be called a "spiritual Pelagianism", telling us everything we were to do, and not mentioning what God was supposed to do.

Pope John saw things differently and believed in a new era, when God's action and gifts would once more come forward. In my final seminary years we were praying for a "new Pentecost in our day".

I didn't know what that meant. I do now. It means I seek first of all God's actions within me.

2. *Realizing Something Is Missing*

Over and again, I see the look in priests' eyes, when they say "will you pray over me". That look says, "I want to meet and experience Jesus Christ because all my life I've served Him and talked about Him, but all along I have never known Him". The experience happens often at our Philadelphia Charismatic Conference for Priests.

At that time, special teachings are given for those new to the Charismatic Movement. This past year we divided the 30 new priests into 3 groups. As I sat down with my ten priests, I asked them why they were at the conference. For every one of them the reason was the same. They all knew someone, lay or clerical, who seemed to have some relationship with Jesus Christ that they didn't have. They knew something was missing.

It is important for the priest to realize that something is missing. The priest can't say, "I have the Church, and I have the

Eucharist and I have the priesthood." He has to say, "Even though I have all these riches (and they are from God), none of them can excuse me from knowing Jesus." In other words, the priest should experience God. No Church can do for the priest what he alone must do — seek the fullness of being God's son in Jesus.

> *"If only you recognized God's gift, and who it is that is asking you for a drink, you would have asked him instead, and he would have given you living water."* (John 4:10)

The gift isn't given "somewhere along the line". It isn't given by putting in so many years in the priesthood. The gift is given at a moment when the priest realizes something is missing.

3. Pain Before The Gift

One time a priest theologian attended a symposium on Charismatic Renewal because a friend asked him to come. So, purely out of friendship, and with absolutely no interest, the priest went.

The speakers were very prominent Church theologians who, instead of giving prepared papers, ended up telling their own personal stories of meeting Jesus in religious experiences.

The priest sat through the whole symposium thinking, "What lousy theology this is". Yet, at the end, a tremendous desire overtook him, since he realized that these theologians had something he didn't have — a personal relationship with Jesus Christ.

In near anger, he demanded that they pray over him. They reluctantly did and nothing happened — at least externally. The months went by, and the priest one day found himself with people who knew something about inner healing, or healing of painful memories. The same angry urge came upon him, followed by the same need and demand for prayer. The people acceded to his request. After that prayer, were released powerful feelings of a deep religious experience.

The priest was a Jesuit, ordained a long number of years. Yet, these two moments of prayer released gifts that were untapped by 30 day retreats, hours of meditation, and years of spiritual exercises.

The secret lay in the simplicity. The priest realized he had never met Jesus and others had.

Jesus is the only door to Christian religious experiences. The only way to enter the door is through the pain, the helplessness, the emptiness of knowing that to know Jesus is everything and realizing the gift hasn't been given yet.

4. I've Tried Everything Else

Since in 1971, few priests were involved in Charismatic Renewal, it was natural for many lay people to come for spiritual advice. I had guided people before, but these people were different. All of these people had received a religious experience. As they described the gift, it dawned on me that this was the gift given to me in June 1954. It had been a life-changing gift. Now there seemed to be a name for it — The Baptism of the Spirit — and it seemed to be mass-produced with everyone speaking of "experiencing God."

As I went around giving talks on religious experiences, many would come up afterwards and speak of their own personal religious experience. One unforgettable talk was to a group of 25 college students whom I wasn't sure were "really buying the message". Hesitantly, as the prepared talk was finished, I opened up the floor for questions. A young girl of 21 quickly jumped up and began, "You heard what Father said — well, you better believe all of it." She then told her story — Catholic background, then falling away, then every kind of sin and finally ready to commit suicide, until a young man spoke to her of Jesus Christ and of asking Jesus to come into her life.

Her response was "Well, I tried everything else, I might as well try Jesus Christ". She sat down and asked, together with the young man, that Jesus come into her life. At that moment, she had the beginning religious experience, was freed of addiction and two years later was back to Church and back to her studies in nursing.

Everywhere I went, I saw that God was multiplying this gift for everyone to have.

5. Go To The Right House

A priest was asked to bless a house where various phenomenon, like ghosts, were occurring. When he returned, the other priest asked him how he handled it. The priest had been so afraid of the phenomenon that he had gone in the house next door and blest the other house from there.

Religious experiences have only one door, Jesus. Everything else, no matter how much it says about prayer or tries to help the priest with prayer, is still only the house next door.

To pray is to meet Jesus, just as to swim is to be in water. Religious experiences begin with the desire to meet Jesus. The first stage culminates when the priest has met Jesus, and knows what it feels like to meet Jesus. So, if you haven't met Jesus and you don't know what it's like to meet Jesus, then you haven't had the beginning religious experiences.

The secret to religious experiences is to start right away with Jesus. Spiritual books leave the impression that a personal meeting with Jesus is "down the road, certainly not the beginning". In truth, the step of meeting Jesus is not "down the road", it is the road. If you haven't met Jesus, you haven't yet begun the road of religious experiences.

Here, helplessness is important. Meeting Jesus is a pure gift. A priest can meditate with his own powers. He can, in a sense, even "pray" with his own powers. But no one will claim that he can meet Jesus with his own power.

Jesus has to come, just as Jesus came to the apostles in the visions. In fact, the visions are the basis of knowing that Jesus will come. Through the visions and the apostles' preaching, we know Jesus is risen from the dead, clothed in immortality and therefore, able to meet us wherever and whenever He chooses.

Don't complicate everything by prayer systems. Seek the gift in Jesus. Go to the right house.

6. The Wrong Type of Pain

In the seminary, we were always taught to be individuals — self-reliant, and self sustaining. American culture praised "being secure" and "being in control."

However, in religious experiences, there is pain and helplessness before the gift.

Priests talk about the pain of the priesthood, the loneliness, and the absence of God. Often the pain they speak of is fruitless, the result of moods, or self-pity or drifting.

The pain described here is of a gift as yet unreceived; an opening inside that waits to be filled with God. The pain itself is the beginning touch of God, the moment of invitation into religious experiences. The receiving comes soon after, as the beginning gift is quickly given.

Leave the God of absence to the philosophers — our God has drawn near to us in Jesus.

Part Two

*Religious
Experiences
and Change*

There'll Be Some Changes Made

After my initial religious experiences in 1954, many psychological changes resulted. Later I discovered that these same changes are always found when the person remains faithful to the gift.

As the experiences continued, self-awareness expanded and caused a basic shift in self-image.

I had always seen myself as good, generous, God-loving, fair, industrious and really successful, even spiritually. The religious experiences showed me whole areas where these were really superficial judgments. The new light wasn't condemnatory, just revealing. I returned to the seminary in September 1954, a much better seminarian, yet thinking much more lowly of myself than the previous year. There was much more charity in my opinion of others.

Changes happened — the deep changes of the Spirit's fruits — peace, patience, kindness, long-suffering. All resulting from the gift of experiencing the Spirit.

This growth stage of religious experiences is usually marked by intense, overwhelming, quickly bestowed experiences, which should lead to life-changing decisions and results. When the initial growth period is over, the priest realizes that God has brought about significant changes. Although the sweeping religious emotions are no longer present, the quiet flame of a taste for prayer remains.

The following chapters describe and encourage the changes resulting from religious experiences.

4

Primary and Secondary Experiences

On either side of the river grew the trees of life which produce fruit twelve times a year, once each month; their leaves serve as medicine for the nations. (Rev. 22:2)

Let us, then, go beyond the initial teaching about Christ and advance to maturity, not laying the foundation all over again. (Heb. 6:1)

God starts anywhere He wants. For clarity sake, I personally divide religious experiences into primary and secondary. The primary religious experience is of Jesus and is described by various phrases, "a prayer gift", a "prayer experience", a "personal knowledge of Jesus", "getting to know Jesus and not just about Him". a "sense of God's presence". All these phrases describe the beginning religious experience – a personal coming to know Jesus through the inner touch of the Spirit.

By "secondary religious experiences" are meant all the other touches of God upon the person.

They include:

1)   A sense of God's closeness.
2)   A renewed faith in God.
3)   A new hope in God's care.
4)   A desire to read Scripture.
5)   Enlightenment about needed changes.
6)   A new power to conquer moral failures.
7)   New understanding of relationship especially within the family, or among working companions.
8)   Desire to serve others, especially in the context of the Church.

Naturally, such a list could be extended, since, descriptions of these secondary experiences are multiple.

Religious experiences are a release of God's power. This release touches the psychological faculties. Since each priest's make-up varies, God begins differently with each individual.

For many, the primary religious experience is also the first one the person receives – they have been "born again", "baptized in the Spirit", or any other name that many call it. These primary experiences have to seep into the other aspects of life so the secondary experiences result.

Others have the secondary religious experiences first, and then later come to know Jesus in a personal way. Priests should not just be content to experience spiritual changes in themselves. They should hunger and thirst to see Jesus, who is doing the work in them.

The following stories try to describe both the primary and secondary changes involved in the personal religious experience.

1. Please Sign My Book

One time we gathered people to review their spiritual progress since their initiation into religious experiences.

One man in my group, a truckdriver, mentioned that since that initiation, he had read the whole New Testament. Then he had gotten hold of this book which he wanted me to sign since I had been such a help. He loved the book because it told him all about the various parts of the Trinity. The book he was enjoying so much, was Sheeban's "Dogmatic Theology"!

The power of religious experiences results in "awakenings" to many divine actions, even to the inner life of the Trinity, so that even a truck driver can enjoy a theological description of the Trinity.

2. "Something Has Happened To You"

A few weeks after getting involved in Charismatic Renewal, I went over to visit a close priest friend. As soon as I started to talk, he said to me "Something has happened to you."

I had always been a "happy person" for whom there were no significant mood shifts, yet the priest was right. The events of the previous weeks had given me an overwhelming enthusiasm about God's activity. Since then, that enthusiasm has remained.

It is not an emotional spiritual high, but is firmly rooted in a faith experience of Jesus Christ. The fruits of that daily experience are:

1) A realization that nothing – no person, event or circumstance can overcome me when the power of Jesus is present.
2) A wisdom that tries to see all events as Jesus sees them.
3) A belief that Jesus will equip me with the needed powers of ministry.

Slowly, since that night, the priest himself has been caught up in religious experiences and he, too, now shares my enthusiasm. Now I can look at him and say, "Something has happened to you."

3. The Caring God

A month ago, we had a large charismatic conference which included about twenty different seminars. For the past two weeks I've been listening to the tapes of those talks.

The stories of the speakers are strikingly similar. A moment of desperation, preceded by the failure of all human means, was followed by a feeling of complete helplessness and a crying out to the Lord. Very quickly, something happened to each one, usually through another person. This answer to prayer caused a whole new understanding of God — as close, dependable and caring.

For one man, this was caused by a business failure. Filled with anxiety, he awoke at night and started to cry as he knelt to pray. He had no more finished the shortest of prayers, than he heard a voice saying "What can I do to help?" It was his wife, awakened from her sleep, and there to help begin a new life.

In a different seminar, it was a prayer in chapel, again a voice at the end of the prayer from a person who had just walked in.

The reality of those moments and those prayers are seen most clearly in the results. The people enjoy a daily life of prayer and now stand in front of many others to proclaim that God always cares in every situation.

Religious experiences are not just feelings. They give the priest a lasting trust in the caring God.

4. King Of The Mountain

In June 1971, I went on our diocesan priest retreat with the firm resolve that I wasn't going to talk about my recent involvement in Charismatic Renewal.

However, some priests had already heard. On the final night, a few began to ask questions. As the explanations were given, especially about the gift of religious experiences, one priest saw further down the road. "I don't want to get involved in this, because if I accept what you're saying then I will have to stop being the King of the Mountain, and I'm not ready to stop."

The priest was tremendously perceptive, because the purpose of religious experiences is to make Jesus the King of the Mountain.

The basic theology of original sin states clearly that we will always make ourselves king unless God's power saves us and installs Jesus as King.

The religious experiences described here are rooted in Christian Baptism and are connected with the risen humanity of Jesus, who is now Lord of all history. These experiences are supposed to make Jesus the Lord of the person who receives them.

5. I'm Into Yoga

I had been asked to speak on Charismatic Renewal to a large group at a Catholic retreat house. Among other things, I mentioned the laying on of hands as a help to experiencing Jesus. This young man came up afterward and asked if I would impose hands on him. It was a sincere request. Before beginning I asked him where he was at, feeling that he had to be connected with some prayer group. His reply surprised me, "I'm into Yoga." I then asked him what his idea was of laying on of hands. "When you lay hands on my head, then all the world power goes through your body and into my body" he replied. "Well, what is your idea of Jesus Christ?" I asked. "He is one of many good people in the world's history", he replied.

I had to tell him that I could not lay hands, since the purpose of the basic religious experiences was to install Jesus as Lord and King.

These experiences are not just psychological phenomena — they are rooted in the historical person of Jesus of Nazareth, the Word made Flesh.

> And no one can say: "Jesus is Lord" except in the Holy Spirit.   (1 Cor 12:3)

6. Reserving The Center For Jesus

In the late 1960's, when everything was breaking loose in the Church, I was in the Chancery Office. One group, among the many that made their way to the office, stood out. Being fed various facts about life inside the rectory by the curate, they were particularly upset about their pastor, and were filled with hostility especially since the "case" was so clear that the pastor should be removed.

A few years later, I met a man from the group. He was changed with an entirely different attitude. I asked what happened. He responded "Well, I experienced Jesus and then I realized that the way I saw the problems wasn't entirely true." The pastor was still there, yet the person was now attending daily mass with no hostility.

For certain priests, hostility feelings predominate as they bristle their way through life. The feelings are usually fed by the intellect that sees everything from a very biased position, forcing the data into a given conclusion, even though the truth shouldn't always lead there.

The priest can think he has so many reasons to be angry — his bishop doesn't care; his pastor is selfish; he is overworked and overlooked; his talents aren't recognized — the litany of anger is endless. It is just as fruitless and harmful.

When Jesus becomes central, the focus shifts. The priest has that important, primary insight that each problem has its place, but the place isn't the center of his whole world. That place is reserved for Jesus.

7. A New Heart

Late last night, I was talking to the assistant pastor when the rectory bell rang. As he went to answer it, I went into my room. Then I realized he probably would appreciate some support. It's a realization that I wouldn't have had a few years ago. I wandered down and the man was giving him a hard time. He appreciated my thoughtfulness and was soon able to resolve the problem.

Religious experiences don't move a priest into a vacuum. They aren't meant to numb the priest so he just accepts everything. The experiences should sensitize the priest to become aware of situations. — the help he needs; the human support he should give; the decision he should be making.

By religious experiences the priest places himself in God's hands and God places into the priest's hands a whole new understanding. This understanding, that leads to quite different decisions, new wisdom and deep, emotional changes, is essential. Otherwise, religious experiences remain surface events.

5

Religious Experiences and Scripture

Likewise, from your infancy you have known the sacred Scriptures, the source of the wisdom which through faith in Jesus Christ leads to salvation.
(2 Tim 3:15)

Its members (in Beroea) were better disposed than those in Thessalonica, and welcomed the message with great enthusiasm. Each day they studied the Scriptures to see whether these things were so.
(Acts 17:11)

A religious experience of the living God is always associated with the inspired word of the same living God. God never changes. What He was doing 2000 years ago, He is doing today.

But that is the trick. If God is not doing anything to you today, then what He did 2000 years ago won't mean much either.

Religious experiences and Scripture are related like hunger to food, and thirst to drink.

A janitor might work in a library all his life and never open a book. A priest can have that library called the bible available in every possible translation, but never be moved to open it.

Religious experiences change all that, bestowing a special taste for God's word, which, in turn, keeps alive and nourishes the experiences. The following stories try to show the link between religious experiences and a love for God's word.

They also explain the secret of the Fundamentalist Churches who know that "being born again" bestows a hunger for God's word.

1. The Name Of The Confederation

At lunch with some younger priests, they were discussing their seminary scripture course and how much they learned of Jewish history and culture — so much so that a visiting Rabbi was totally shocked by their knowing the name for the confederation of tribes.

The seminary course has changed and new doors of understanding are opened, but what does that mean without religious experiences?

Knowing the long name for the confederation of tribes, doesn't bestow the power to feed the priest or the people. It isn't just by knowledge that the word of God nourishes.

Almost every day I spend time with Scriptural commentaries, but that level of understanding is as nothing compared to the Scriptures read in the light of religious experiences.

2. Still In The Box

In 1963, during a high school CCD class, I asked the students if they had a family bible. One young man quickly raised his hand, "My parents have this beautiful bible they got at their wedding and its still in the box."

"Still in the box" probably sums up where many Catholic bibles are. Providing commentaries, printing new editions, making up-to-date translations are all helps in bringing the Bible closer. However, actually drinking demands first an inner thirst.

Sometimes, we priests can see the "born-again Churches" as "bible-banging", and the people as "bible-carrying". Really, we should be jealous of those Churches and seek out how they get people to read the bible.

The core answer is a religious experience. A person who experiences God wants to read the bible.

The Catholic Church has sought Scriptural Renewal. We have had better vernacular translations; more stress on the Liturgy of the Word; more Scriptural guides and commentaries. However, the Church doesn't yet seem to grasp that Scripture is a very personal book. The only door to Scripture is a personal religious experience. It is Jesus who makes people thirst for His Word.

When people come to know Jesus, then they begin to look up the good translations and get out the latest commentaries. The religious experience comes first. Love for Scripture quickly follows. Without religious experience, no full devotion to Scripture can exist.

If the Catholic Church wants true Scriptural Renewal, it has to commit itself to fostering religious experiences.

3. Pro-Football Bible Bangers

With the Philadelphia Eagles going to the Super Bowl, the papers are filled with every possible background story. Today's story dealt with the defensive backfield, all of whom have experienced Jesus Christ and gather every Monday night for bible study. The article contrasted their lockers, which always have well-worn bibles, and the decorations on the other lockers.

Often, during the season, these players have openly mentioned their devotion to Jesus Christ, and how much He has meant to all of them. Also, in a few years, the group has grown from just three players to twelve.

The article showed pro-football players turning to Jesus Christ for help, and having bibles that are well-used and marked up. The story also shows a normal three-part experience:

1) The personal religious experience of Jesus.
2) Following upon that experience, a desire to learn about Jesus in Scripture.
3) The desire to tell others the good news and invite them into this new life.

The tremendous power in that approach is manifested everywhere, even in pro-football locker rooms!

4. Figure It Out For Yourselves

One time, as were coming from our usually perplexing scripture class, a seminarian made the statement, "The greatest mystery of Christianity is that God put revelation into a bible and then said 'Here it is everybody, now try to figure it out for yourselves.'"

At the time, the early 1960's, there was a disparity between the theology courses, where everything was so clear with "pre-packaged", well defined truths (with the proper theological note), and the scripture courses where even the most simple statement somehow wasn't that simple, "If God wanted to reveal, why didn't He do it through a theology book, rather than a very confused bible?", I used to think.

Now, I don't think that way, because the bible stories are something I live. If a priest is immersed in religious experiences, he will recognize in scripture his own experiences with God.

Power in the priesthood doesn't come from applying theological principles but by living out scriptural examples.

So I walk now in a different light — no longer by the sun of theology but by the brilliant light of scriptural living. Protection comes from theology, but power comes from the ever-active God of the Scriptures.

5. *Jesus Is Here*

When we were children, the family would gather for the rosary. Afterwards, my mother would say "Jesus is here". I would ask her how He was here and she would say "Well, Scripture says, *'Where two or more are gathered in my name, I am present.'"*

As I grew up, I realized that mom was right — Jesus was truly present just as Scripture said.

Religious experiences bestow a scriptural faith. They mold our minds according to the living God of the scriptures. There is only one God — the God of the scriptures. There is only one real picture of a life with God — the life in the scriptures. So, now the scriptures live within me.

Sometimes scriptural living is striking. A group of priests all approaching forty, were having a day of prayer. At lunch the conversation turned to changes that happened when a person turns forty. On the way home with another priest, I opened the Scripture to Acts C4, the healing of the lame man. I never before realized V22 read "The fact was, the man thus miraculously cured was more than forty years of age."

6. *A Taste For Scripture*

One Sunday during my homily, I wanted to read some passage from Scripture, so I brought my bible over to the sacristy. As I got ready to go out with the altar boys, I found myself very self-conscious. I was actually going to go to the altar carrying the bible! The humor in the whole situation only heightened as I went out into the congregation. I found myself shifting the bible from one hand to the other, and the people themselves looking somewhat mystified — "Why is Father carrying a bible?" The whole situation is à clear picture of the absence of Scripture in daily reading.

The secret of giving people a love for Scripture is not good bible classes (they are an effect), but of getting people personally in touch with the author. True religious experiences always lead to a desire to read Scripture (after all, an author always wants to sell his book).

Every priest for whom religious experiences are important also has a desire for Scripture (and many of them even carry the bible, or have one in the car). Religious experiences are the key to unlock the Scriptural world.

6

Overcoming Addictions

Therefore reform your lives! Turn to God, that your sins may be wiped away! Thus may a season of refreshment be granted you by the Lord when he sends you Jesus, already designated as your Messiah. (Acts 3:19-20)

It is true he was crucified out of weakness, but he lives by the power of God. We too are weak in him, but we live with him by God's power in us.
(2 Cor 13:4)

Introduction

With ordination, the seminary discipline slips into the past. Unfortunately, with years in the priesthood, many other things slip into our lives – not necessarily "sinful things" just the "perks" of priesthood, what is called "priestly life-style".

Religious experiences have to change a disordered life-style, or else those experiences die out. God's gift should enter deeply into the priest, drawing him away from what he clings to.

By His nature, God rightly claims everything as His own. Religious experiences and a priest's addiction are incompatible. At some point one of them goes.

When the addiction goes, a new level of experience and power result. Often, this freeing action of God is much greater than the beginning gift because now the priest is learning how to yield to God.

The gradual giving up of addictions clears the field so the Lord can build the house.

Priestly addictions are legion – sports, television, movies, alcohol, oversmoking, sexuality. With the freedom from family cares and children, a priest's life is particularly prone to these addictions.

Some are incompatible with priesthood, and the priest knows he is living a double life. Other addictions, which can be just as devastating, ruin an entire priesthood.

Religious experiences are flood-like, uprooting addictions and leaving the priest free for the first time in years.

The following stories touch on the familiar addictions – those possibly present in any priest's life.

1. The Movie Page

The following is a story of a growing addiction that had to be stopped.

A priest felt his job had a lot of pressures. Since he was so faithful to it, and to many other preaching engagements, he also felt that he had a right to a regular movie.

After a while the weekly movie became twice a week. He daily found himself looking through the movie ads. Since the week was crammed with work, nothing seemed too wrong in this arrangement. Two other factors occurred — the priest obviously had to go out alone, since the decision for the movie often was made at the last minute — and, since the number of good movies is limited, many times he found himself going to movies that were questionable.

Movies became an addiction that made the priest superficial in his ministry.

Religious experiences changed that. First, there was the gradual resolve to avoid questionable movies. Then his frequency in attending died down, and finally the frenzied search through the movie pages passed away.

Every priest has addictions that unfortunately have taken root. Many are incompatible with priesthood. Yet the gift of religious experiences shows the priest how he should be free of them. The priest must yield to that gift.

2. The Nicotine Problem

One priest told me his rather remarkable story. He was reading a book on healing, and specifically a chapter on freedom from smoking. He was reading, as always, with a cigarette in hand. He had tried often to stop. In the middle of the chapter, he put out the cigarette and never again had even the desire to smoke.

Other stories are less dramatic, but with the same result. Religious experiences simplify priestly life-style. In place of addictions, come gifts of personal growth and ministry.

3. Johnny Walker

One time, we were at a diocesan workshop for priests, and the speaker was talking about the problems of loneliness and of going back to a rectory where nobody was there to greet you. A priest sitting nearby made a comment for all around to hear "What do you mean nobody to greet me? Johnny Walker is always in my room to greet me!"

I know the priest well. He is not an alcoholic. That he could freely joke about Johnny Walker, showed he wasn't trying to cover up a problem. What he was uncovering was a reality — how often a priest can be greeted by alcohol.

Alcohol can substitute for many things. Problems can result even when the priest is not an alcoholic —fitful sleep, high salt, high blood pressure, the tendency to depend on the warmth and good feeling flowing from the bottle.

Religious experiences inevitably clash with alcohol dependency, causing the priest to face honestly his addiction.

4. Television

When religious experiences become central, the priest begins limiting his television watching. On the other hand, priests who have never faced the problem of television's pervasiveness have never been able to foster these experiences.

The reason is obvious — fostering religious experiences demands time be set aside to allow the intervention of God. Television is like a sponge, always threatening to absorb every available moment.

In my own priesthood, as the gift of religious experiences grew, television watching faded more and more into the background.

On the evening before the Feast of Christ the King, I was trying to write my sermon. Unfortunately, a basketball game was on television that night. So the evening was spent writing the sermon and turning the television on to find out the score.

The next morning's review of my sermon notes caused a great deal of dissatisfaction. The reason was all too obvious. So, on the feast of Christ the King, 1978, my old, portable black and white television was moved to the rectory attic, where it is to this day. With that transition, Jesus became the Lord of my room. The gifts of prayer and reading come easier now.

Yesterday, I realized the important effects of that decision. The five priests, comprising the Tribunal staff, used a near-empty Jersey-shore motel to evaluate our work. The day's work concluded with dinner. As we returned to the motel, two priests came to my room to watch Monday night football. After the first half, they went to bed. I had visions of a nice sleep beginning around 10:30 P.M.

However, after washing up for bed, I flicked the switch back on. The rest of the story is common to all of us. At midnight I was still glued to the set and 12:30 A.M. found me trying to get myself settled down, instead of deeply asleep.

I realized again the tremendous temptation to flip on the switch when the television is in the room.

5. Addicted To Ideas

A nurse once asked me to speak with her boy friend. He was a tremendous person but confused. He had been in the seminary; then in the peace corps. Now he was thinking of going away to some other volunteer group. His problem was obvious — he was dominated by unrealistic ideas. These ideas had to be shattered so he could be free to be truly the person God intended. So I spent an hour shattering those ideas. The couple are now happily married.

Many priests have ideas that dominate and bind them. A priest feels called to a work that really is not for him; feels he has talent that is being overlooked; feels he has to serve way beyond his capacity; feels success in priesthood is tied up with Church ranking or position; feels his ideas should have a bigger forum; feels his work should have a better stage. The ideas that can cause bondage are multiple. As long as they "tick" inside the priest, his life and ministry will always be flawed.

These ideas never let the priest be free. He is addicted to them. He can't take himself and his world as it is and begin from there. A priest who lets go of a false idea, experiences a real freedom from a true addiction.

7

Experiences - Religious and Human

This treasure we possess in earthen vessels.
(2 Cor 4:7)

. . . He who pierces the heart, bares its feelings. . .
(Sirach 22:19)

This is not a psychology chapter inserted to ward off objections that "feelings" aren't discussed or a human approach to God is removed by placing so much stress on God's gift of religious experiences.

A whole book would be needed for that.

Modern teachings say "Get in touch with your feelings". Since religious experiences deal very much in feelings, three points are clear;

1) Awareness of religious feelings towards God, should also bring awareness of personal feelings to others.
2) Religious enlightenment demands, and bestows, human enlightenment.
3) Religious and human experiences should interact, supporting and clarifying each other.

After eight years of working with priests, many of us have come to some conclusions.

1) A regular seeking for and experiencing of God's presence affects a priest on human levels.
2) A fidelity to religious experiences makes the priest more normal emotionally, and reduces relationship problems.
3) Any priest can be helped in these areas.
4) Religious experiences awaken the priest to problems that everyone else knew he had, and frequently leads the priest to seek the human help of counseling.

All the stories in this book deal with human experiences. The following, however, seem to deal directly with the need to "be in touch with what is happening".

1. A Summer Course

One time a religious sister came for prayers. She taught math and had signed up for yet another summer math course. As I prayed with her, I had the sense that the decision was wrong. Not knowing much about her or her background, I then asked her to discuss the problem.

She was teaching at the grade school level and had already finished her math work. However, she felt duty bound to continue to strive and take more math courses for the good of the students.

However, God wanted her to take courses for her own enrichment. She said that she felt personally deficient in theology, and would enjoy studying theology.

Since then much has happened. A small decision — the nature of a summer course — was really very basic, for it touched the core of her being. Was God somebody who only wanted her to strive or was God someone who delighted in her enjoying?

Since then, much has unravelled — often painfully. Today she is freer, more balanced, and a much better religious, because of making a basic decision in the light of a religious experience.

2. Not Just A "Pious Time"

Religious experiences light up a lot of the priest's hidden world — hidden even from himself. When feelings towards God are released, then light begins to shine on a lot of so-called "natural problems."

Basic decisions have to be made and this is a key part of the growth stage. If the priest, a year after he begins to experience God sees no basic problems or questions, and has not been led to some basic decisions about shifts in his life, then the experiences have been of little help and probably will die out quickly. He will then see religious experiences as a certain "pious time" in his priesthood that is now past.

3. Having Someone To Speak The Truth

Our prayer group contained a number of religious sisters from the same community. Since one of these sisters was older, had been a superior, and was deepest into the spiritual gifts, the others looked to her for guidance. Gradually, without causing an "elitist" group, the sisters came closer and closer together.

However, everything wasn't just peaches and cream. Religious experiences didn't cover over or take away the human problems.

Fortunately, honest words were said. Problems were faced. No beating around the bush. Many tears were shed (not in vain) but the sisters grew stronger in the honesty.

Each sister has learned much, and changed much. They accepted the honest gift of truth at each crossroad. The safeguard, even for the future, is the painful telling of the truth.

The above story uncovers many flaws in priestly experience:

1) Most priest lead isolated lives.
2) Most priests, if they even have religious experiences, don't share this or themselves with others.
3) Most priests don't have anyone who can give them needed words of truth.
4) Most priests don't even have anyone who knows them well enough to give the needed words of truth.

Yet words from someone who knows us, loves us, and shares with us the experience of Jesus Christ, are absolutely essential to spiritual growth.

4. Discerning Situations

Just yesterday a priest came about a decision. We had talked a few months previously and felt that at some point a change in his ministry would have to be sought.

The whole process was hastened by a ten-day hospitalization. This made him realize that he had to change his present high school assignment. He came to ask what I thought. I told him that I would have wanted the change earlier but that he was still holding on. Fortunately the hospitalization had done what I didn't feel I should do — get him to see the need for a change.

The priest then talked about his prayer. The gift of religious experiences began three years ago. This past summer, he would join us at the priest prayer group. He said he couldn't understand why God seemed so close to him during the summer and so far away as September came and school began again. Two months later he was in the hospital.

The story typifies a major point about religious experiences — namely, the need to discern daily experience. The priest has to keep his eyes open about what is happening to him every day and in every circumstance.

The rectory, the work, his parents and family, his health — the priest has to look carefully at all of these regularly.

5. The Body And Booze

The other night, before the priest prayer meeting, a priest mentioned how much he has curtailed his alcoholic intake. The priest is not an alcoholic, but the story was an all too common one.

The other priest would invite him to a drink before dinner. One would become two and the occasional invitation became a daily one. The priest noticed a loss of appetite and difficulty in sleeping.

Many vocational and living factors open the priest to alcoholic problems (even when the priest is in no way "an alcoholic").

1) Most priests don't go "out to work" but have the emotionally unsound situation that they live and work in the same place.
2) Most priests, free of spouse and children, are able to be alone for long periods, and are expected to be alone at night.
3) Drinking is a quite acceptable part of rectory living and even fostered as a "good source of community".

Religious experiences should lead the priest to examine his life-style. He must be willing to be honest about every situation. A serious question for many is the relationship to alcohol.

Since prayer meetings are at night, we stress that no alcohol be consumed before the meeting. Also religious experiences lessen the need for the consolation from other spirits.

Most of all, religious experiences cannot grow and flourish in a body where the arteries, veins, brain and nervous systems are frequently touched by the power of alcohol.

Part Three

Reflecting On
Religious
Experiences

It is not enough to say "This is happening and that is happening". A legitimate question arises, "Just what is this and that which are supposedly happening?" True reflection provides a basis for experiences, and allows the mind to yield to the heart.

Legitimate questions surround religious experiences. Experiences, without reflection, theology and tradition provide a very unsure foundation.

The following chapters offer some basic reflections on the foundations of this book's teachings. "Reflections on experiences" in a scientific way is theology. Systematic theology tries to raise every possible question and arrive at definite conclusions based on proof. In these chapters the "reflections on experiences" are quite different.

The goal is to have the priest think to himself:
1. "There seems to be something here."
2. "There is a new era."
3. "Something is going on."
4. "There is a new power in the Church."
5. "We are experiencing a 'new Pentecost'."
6. "My priesthood can really be changed."
7. "Maybe there is still hope for all the dreams I once had."

I don't apologize that these chapters don't provide "complete and systematic proof" about the nearness of the unknown God. Paul tried that and received only the intellectual response,

"We must hear you on this topic some other time"
(Acts 17:32)

At some other time, I'll try to provide the systematic proof. But for now, just simple chapters, so the mind can at least follow the heart a little bit.

8

The New Era

Every scribe who is learned in the reign of God is like the head of a household who can bring from his storeroom both the new and the old.

(Matt. 13:52)

The One who sat on the throne said to me "See, I make all things new!"   (Rev. 21:5)

Concerning this book the priest can easily ask, "If all of this is true, then where has the Church been all these years?" He can even question what he himself has accomplished in his priesthood.

Many times, I have asked myself the same questions. When I write all these things, it seems like a new world, like a different Church.

The only conclusion I can come to is that we are in a new era; that God is doing something new and special. I don't totally understand it, but God wants this book written now even though the new era is only beginning.

I feel like Habakuk:

> *"Then the Lord answered me and said: Write down the vision clearly upon the tablets, so that one can read it readily. For the vision still has its time, presses on to fulfillment, and will not disappoint; If it delays, wait for it, it will surely come, it will not be late."* (2:3)

What these stories say is, "The vision is not late. It does not delay, and will not disappoint, because we are in a new era."

1. The Seminary Years

I was asked by a priest to speak to a home prayer group that he was beginning. The talk was on Charismatic Renewal, since those in the group knew nothing about the Movement.

Afterward the priest shared with me his own spiritual beginnings. His years in the seminary had never really taught him to pray. However, toward the end of those years he had come across a group of lay people who prayed together on a regular basis. By joining with them, the priest received the gift of prayer. He found himself in the awkward position of leaving the seminary grounds to learn how to pray!

The story contains two important lessons. First, the years in the seminary might be spiritually fruitless, even though much time is given to prayer exercise. Secondly, the prayer gift is not that far away from any priest, if he just seeks it directly.

But the real reason for hope (and for not blaming the seminary) is the new era. What I have seen, and experienced, personally and through others, was unthinkable twenty years ago. The frequency and intensity of God's prayer gifts are quantitatively and qualitatively different than twenty years ago. We are in a new age and the entire priesthood is offered the Davidic anointing.

2. You Have Discovered Something New

Many times in the seminary, others would come and ask me how I prayed. I would try to explain, but the explanation was so simple that I am sure they received little help.

In those days, there was very little talk about religious experiences because basically they were seen as a private matter — personal gifts that God gave to special type people.

In 1973, I attended a theology symposium on religious experiences. A theologian, deeply committed to the widescale spread of these experiences, presented a paper claiming the theological basis of religious experiences were the "freely given gifts" of St. Thomas Aquinas. According to him, these experiences were theologically the same as the gifts of martyrdom or a religious vocation, namely, given to some but not for all.

A dialogue ensued in which others argued that to make these experiences only for some would sidetrack this widespread action of God.

Fortunately, I rode to the airport in the same taxi with the theologian and we continued the dialogue. I pointed out that our theology links these religious experiences to Baptism and therefore for everyone.

He saw the implication immediately, "If that is true" he said, "then you have discovered a teaching about Baptism that the Church has overlooked for 1900 years."

The important point is not if the Church has or has not overlooked the teaching. What is important is the widespread scale of God's bestowal of religious experiences and our grasping the central (Baptismal) importance of these experiences.

3. Kneeling Before The Television

One time a priest called and asked if I would talk to a parishioner. He said that she had had a religious experience, which he felt was valid, but it was mixed in with other confusing elements.

Later, the woman called and told her story. She said she watched the Protestant television programs and always laughed at them. One night, after her husband had gone to bed, she was watching as the television preacher invited everybody to kneel down and accept Jesus as Lord.

Strangely enough, this time she didn't laugh, but instead made sure her family was asleep and then knelt down. Right there in her living room! Before the television screen with a Protestant minister! The result was a very special religious experience, that had begun then and seemed to be perduring. She spent some time describing what she had done, how the gift began and what had happened to her since.

What she described so accurately to me was the beginning religious experience — the first definable effect of the Lordship that Jesus claimed over her in Baptism. The gift was received in a very normal traditional way — the preaching of the message. (The only new aspect was the use of modern television.)

All of these chapters can only go that far — preaching the message that Baptism contains the power of religious experiences. The priest has to kneel down and ask that Jesus come into his heart as Lord of his life. It is a new era. The very mass media that so confuses, is also used by God. Religious experiences are as abundant as television sets.

4. Something's Happened to Me

One night I was asked to give a talk on Charismatic Renewal to a parish group. The first part was explanation followed by a question and answer session.

Afterwards, two women who came together, wanted to talk to me. Both had received the gift of religious experience. One looked at the other and said, "Something has happened to me." The other replied, "Something's happened to me." The description of their individual experiences was again an accurate description of the basic experience of the Lordship of Jesus. My only task was to verify the experiences, help them to pray in tongues and tell them how to follow through.

What is essentially noteworthy was that the evening didn't even include a prayer for the gift. The experiences were given during the question and answer period.

The normal means of receiving the gift is to listen to the message that Jesus wants you to have the gift, and then reach out to receive it.

The era is so new, that even questions and answers can bestow the beginning gift.

5. The Confusing Computer

I picked up my nephew's college book on computers and couldn't make sense of the first page, or any page. When the new math appeared, the question always was "Why replace the old system?"

But there were new realities — and the old system couldn't handle the new complexities. So a new system had to be formulated.

New insights often focus not just on a better use of a present system, but the construction of a wholly new system to handle the new and more complicated problems.

The same holds true for the priesthood. The world presents new complexities and priestly renewal won't result just from making a better use of the present system.

The Church is never committed to its present system. The Church's only committal is to Jesus Christ. Only He is the same yesterday, today and forever.

So, what is Jesus doing in the world? He is always doing a new work. A committal to Jesus involves an openness to the new era.

6. *Searching For The New Church*

A fairly large town outside of Philadelphia was built around two industries. The first left a few years ago, and the second just announced that the plant will be closing. The people are confused as to why this is happening, but the owners are not being "hard-hearted". The industry has changed so much that the type and quality of the product produced at this factory just does not respond to modern needs. Also, unfortunately, the retooling and retraining were put off for so long that it is economically unfeasible to make any effort to keep the plant alive.

Jesus promised His Church's existence to the end of time, but He never promised that no plant in that company would ever go out of business. Unhappily the history of the Church has too many instances of a flourishing Church life that gradually succumbed. Even today, serious questions exist about the vitality of the Church in Western Europe, and no one can feel smug about the future of American Catholicism.

So the questions is – are we priests open to the new era or will a moment come when the only alternative will be the plant's closing?

Not to search for new powers is complete folly in our constantly changing world. If we priests feel that what we have today will suffice for tomorrow, we are just not being faithful to Jesus.

> *"This means that if anyone is in Christ, he is a new creation. The old order has passed away; now all is new."* (Cor 5:17)

9

Theory and Theology

Jesus responded: "You hold the office of teacher of Isreal and still you do not understand these matters?   (Jn. 3:10)

that mystery hidden from ages and generations past but now revealed to his holy ones

(Col. 1:26)

... the gospel which I proclaim when I preach Jesus Christ, the gospel which reveals the mystery hidden for many ages . .   (Rom 16:25)

Any priest with his years of theological training, is never content to just experience or to witness experiences. His mind always seeks to know — "Where does this fit in? Where does it come from? How do these experiences relate to the rest of Catholic teaching?"

The answer, in the form of stories with explanations, is only an outline of needed theological research. Unfortunately, theology (including St. Thomas) has centered so much on the Trinitarian and Christological questions, that little writing has been done on "the apostolic experience" and just what is involved in "receiving the Spirit."

If we cannot understand the stress certain Churches place on "being born again", they certainly cannot understand our preoccupation with theological questions that seem far removed from the personal spiritual needs of the people. So experiences need theory and theology needs experiences.

The following stories touch upon a theory and theology of religious experiences.

1. Theory and Practice

One time, at a workshop, a Jesuit was describing his theory of prayer. I marveled at the theory, because he had developed a vey true plan. The marvel was that he had worked out this theory, but seemingly had never had the beginning experience.

He spoke of salvation in terms of a religious experience, of experiencing a new mode of being, a religious breakthrough. He used the example of learning how to swim, that moment of excitement when the person, for the first time, is staying above the water without having his foot on the bottom of the pool.

Since he was a liturgist, he took the example further. Unless people have this "experience of salvation" as he called it, then going to Eucharist is like a group of nonswimmers celebrating at a swim club.

His theory of religious experience and liturgy was excellent. Unless people have experienced their salvation in Jesus, coming together to celebrate a non-experienced reality is boring and tedious.

However, when he came to describe prayer practice it seemed that the experiences weren't there. The result was that I marveled even more at how he had come up with the theory.

Besides immersing the reader into stories of religious experiences, the theory underlying this book needs a clear statement:

1) A primary gift of Baptism is a religious experience.
2) Every baptized person can and should know Jesus Christ in a personal way through this gift of an initial religious experience.
3) The liturgy, as the communal expression of Baptism, should celebrate a salvation that in some way has been experienced.
4) While the foundation of christian community is faith, an unexperienced faith has little power in holding a community together.

2. Where Do They Come From?

Since 1971, my life has been immersed with people, hundreds and thousands, who have had a personal religious experience.

Early on, I went to some Protestant groups that stressed the same experience. These groups made no attempt to systematize. They let the experiences and the changes in people's lives speak for themselves.

However, this wasn't satisfying, for Catholic theology is always seeking an understanding of religious phenomena. So, I began the theological search to find the answer for myself and to explain to others — "Where do these religious experiences come from?"

The answer, of course, is the Holy Spirit, but the Holy Spirit is too general a response. He is the soul of the Mystical Body, and His power is everywhere — from the ordination of priests to the infallibility of the Pope.

My theological search turned to the sacrament of Baptism. As a Catholic, I had to reject the Protestant teaching that these religious experiences are a salvation event since, for Catholics, salvation begins at Baptism. The Spirit isn't given by the religious experiences. He is given by Baptism.

The theological conclusion was that these experiences were the fruit of Baptism.

Suddenly, my theological mind was racing and certain conclusions came quickly:

1) If religious experiences are the fruit of Baptism, then logically everyone who is baptized, should be enjoying them.

2) If that is true, then a whole new power exists that the Catholic Church never dreamed of.

3) New power would come to the Church by seeking to fully release these Baptismal powers.

4) Priests have a duty, not only to see that their people are baptized, but that they receive the religious experiences associated with Baptism.

Suddenly the whole vista of a renewed Catholic Church was before my eyes. In my own little way, I felt like Paul who saw:

> *that mystery hidden from ages and generations*
> *past but now revealed to his holy ones.*
>
> (Col. 1:26)

The mystery is this:

Baptism contains the seed of religious experiences, and every baptized person has within himself the power to experience God.

Imagine any parish where everyone regularly experienced God. But first — the priest. The vision will never happen in the Catholic Church unless it first happens to the priesthood. This is what the Davidic anointing means.

3. I Know What It Means To Meet Jesus

One evening a priest called and asked if I would go to a near-by hospital where a twelve year old was dying. He had been hit by a car; was officially pronounced dead; but was being kept alive by machines. The story of that night is an extraordinary one, both with the boy and with the members of the family.

On the way to the hospital, after praying to know the Lord's will, I had the sense that the prayers would be answered by the Lord taking the boy without the parents having to make a decision to remove the machines. (This is what happened 3 days later).

After praying over the boy, I went to the waiting room to meet the family. Here the story begins. The father, himself, years before, had suffered a heart attack and had been pronounced dead. During that time he had, what he considered, after-death experiences.

Therefore, when I greeted the family, he told me that he knew what it was like to be dead, and he knew what his son, Michael, was experiencing. He was saying, "I know what it's like to meet Jesus. I know what Michael is experiencing. But I still think, I should never turn the machine off."

He kept saying "I know what it's like to meet Jesus. When you meet Jesus, you never want to come back to earth."

I don't want to comment here on the validity of the so-called "after death experiences". I do want to claim that there is an experience of Jesus that is meant to happen to all of us who are baptized, long before we die. This experience is a primary gift of Baptism and has happened to hundreds of thousands.

Call it "born-again", call it "A salvation experience". Call it any name you want. The experience seems to be for anyone who seeks it.

Long before death, every baptized person should be able to say "I know what it's like to meet Jesus". In traditional theological terms, this teaching represents the opinion that the gift of contemplation is for everyone.

4. How Do They Begin?

Since 1971, life for me has been like a pin ball machine, bouncing back and forth between real life experiences, theory, theology and Scripture and back to experiences.

By 1973, I had worked out the theology of religious experiences as the enlightenment gift rooted in Baptism. This theology was based on the Scriptural examples given in the Acts and presupposed in Romans and Corinthians.

But how can the Church go from theory to practice? What was entailed in releasing the Baptismal gift of religious experiences? I saw thousands of people who experienced God. What brought this about?

There seemed to be a couple of components.

First, A group of people who enjoyed religious experiences would come together publicly and let their worship flow from these experiences.

Second, Others who did not have these experiences, would naturally be led to seek these gifts.

Thirdly, They would then ask for this gift and surrender their lives to Jesus as Lord.

The theory only had three steps. Religious experiences were bestowed at a given moment, in a given place. Everyone had a story of Jesus coming into their lives. As I watched the process over and over again, I would recall my own room, 1954, and the time when Jesus came to me in the gift of religious experiences.

5. *How Long Do They Last?*

In spite of what I saw and heard, one burning question remained within me — How long will these experiences last? Or better — How long will the people be faithful to the gift?

I knew the gift could last, because ever since my own experience in 1954, the prayer gift had remained. But that gift was given to a highly-motivated seminarian who sought God because he wanted to be a priest. The gift was central to what I was going to be, and was nourished for years by seminary discipline, with all the helps of a spiritual guide and planned spiritual exercises.

None of that seemed to be present here. The people were coming from the byways and highways. Some had stopped attending Church before the gift was given. Some were just getting away from addictions. There was nothing here except the power of the religious experience itself, and a few hastily contrived teachings to foster it.

In spite of everything — the experience prevailed. I was suddenly in a topsy-turvey world — where a kid just off mainlining drugs would spend an hour in prayer; where a kid just a few months away from using drugs, was now involved in helping others; where people who had been away from Church, became daily communicants. The greatest sign of all were the regular, steady parishioners who said that they now had a new religious life.

And the experiences lasted! It is now years later and the same people still gather. They remember their first religious experience — the time and place that they experienced the love of Jesus — and they are still faithful to the gift.

10

Validating Religious Experiences

None of those who cry out, "Lord, Lord" will enter the kingdom of God but only the one who does the will of my Father in heaven.

(Matt. 7:21)

Test yourselves to see whether you are living in faith; examine yourselves. (2 Cor 13:5)

Introduction

I had dinner tonight with a close priest friend. In discussing this book, he asked me to handle the question of validating religious experiences. Years ago, he had done a little writing on religious experiences within the Jesuits, sending surveys with very specific questions to forty Jesuits. Now, of these forty, eight have left the priesthood. So just how valid were the experiences? Also, St. Ignatius says that an experience is validated only by its later history, when it can be seen what the experience has done for the person.

Some points should be stated clearly:

1) To have the beginning religious experience is not as difficult as being faithful to this gift for a lifetime. A later spiritual collapse doesn't mean the original experience was invalid. The continuing gift was just not accepted or cooperated with.
2) A beginning religious experience might be valid, but the next steps might not be.
3) If a person is led off the true path, the problem is probably with subsequent experiences, or decisions, or wrong reflections on the experience.

Two distinct questions exist — first, validating the beginning religious experience and second, validating everything spiritual that happened since then.

This chapter can only deal with the first question. The second is already handled well in Catholic spiritual traditions which demand discernment in every decision of the spiritual life.

The important teaching of this book is that an initial religious experience of knowing Jesus Christ in a personal way is a primary result of Baptism and is available to every baptized person.

The following stories touch the basic question of validating initial religious experiences.

1. Surprise – A Gift From God

After speaking with my priest friend, I began to think on my own 1954 religious experiences. I just never bothered to validate the whole thing because I didn't think it was necessary. I was praying faithfully, seeking a life of prayer, and Jesus had given me a gift of His presence. Why try to validate something so simple?

That is probably true of most – the person doesn't even question that the experience is from God. Usually no problem exists in the beginning. The new-born child in the crib is helpless and can only go where his parents put him. So, during the beginning religious experiences most people are helpless.

Real problems occur when the infant is able to crawl and to walk. The same is true of these experiences. When the person has experienced them for a while, and begins to crawl under his own power, validation of religious experiences becomes extremely necessary.

The beginning experiences are so new and so surprising that usually only God could be the source.

2. The Good Confessor

I never questioned the validity of my own experience. They were pure gifts. I knew they came from Jesus, for wasn't I seeking Him?

The problem wasn't with the gift. The problem was what I did with it. The problems were the darkness and confusion from within me. How did I handle this gift of light?

Fortunately, I had a confessor, and for the next eight years of seminary life, everything was placed before him. His advice was extremely important. Since obedience was such a part of me, everything was carefully observed.

In the beginning, the advice always calmed down my fervor. Later, it supported my efforts to persevere in prayer.

It was my confessor who validated my religious experiences. I never really bothered with that question. I knew they were from Jesus.

3. Presuming

Most people never question whether or not the initial religious experience is from God. They are probably right. The reasons are simple — usually they are searching for God, are in a religious atmosphere and usually feel good about the whole thing.

If those conditions aren't met then a question can be raised. For example, Jimmy (The Weasel) Fratiani spoke of his religious feelings as he was initiated into the Cosa Nostra. Questions can be raised about the religious experiences flowing from Yoga, Transcendental Meditation, pantheistic religions, or especially occult practices.

When, however, a person is seeking Jesus Christ and has received sound basic teaching within the Church, then the basic presumption should be that the beginning religious experience is a true gift of Jesus, who wants all the baptized to experience Him.

4. Experiences in Vegas

A young woman had been with our prayer group for a short time, when she and another girl took a Las Vegas vacation.

After a few days of the glittering lights, she was confused and depressed. One day as she was walking down the Strip, she had a religious experience.

During the remaining days and after her return, the experiences continued, but they had put her on a roller coaster.

To this day, I don't know the whole story or the sources of these so-called religious experiences, but a short accounting of what was happening was enough to know they did not come from God.

I just told her to give up the experiences since they were not from God, and to let herself be prayed over for peace. The experiences stopped. The girl now sees clearly that they were invalid religious experiences.

5. Yoga and Confirmation

Just how or where a person first experiences God doesn't always determine the validity of the gift.

One high school girl was sent to me by an anxious religious. The girl had gone to a day of yoga initiation — the incentive type, day long seminars to attract new members.

However, although she had not returned, an experience of the day had remained with her and the religious sister was rightfully concerned about the validity of the experience.

The girl was a delight to speak to. She described what had happened on that day and since. The original experience and the results seemed much the same as happens regularly at prayer groups.

I finally asked her what she felt happened. The answer came right away, "I think I experienced my Confirmation."

The day's teaching might have been about Yoga, but the girl "translated" the teachings according to her Catholic training, and experienced the power of the initiation sacraments.

6. Drugs and Religious Experiences

Many experiences center around drug use and alcohol, although these should not be quickly dismissed as an emotional high.

A girl confided once that she had been involved in drugs, and in fact was on her way to buy some when she called out to God to deliver her. A beginning religious experience came, which not only turned her away from the drug scene but led her to the charitable work of aiding others to freedom.

On another occasion a youth group joined me in giving a presentation to CYO leaders. One boy told his story — a problem of mainlining; an invitation to a prayer meeting; his acceptance mainly to laugh and scoff; but resulting instead in a special gift of God's presence.

Following the presentation, about eight of the leaders asked if they could experience a prayer meeting. Since we had only five minutes before supper, we quickly gathered to pray. After those few minutes, all of the eight CYO leaders were in tears. One kept saying "I'm not that holy, to feel this way." Despite trying to quiet them before dinner, they went into the dining hall and told the other 200 what had happened — and the simple power of the gospel stories was repeated, as others sought to be prayed over.

In all of these cases, the persons thought the gift was from God. They were probably right. The beginning gift, usually a complete surprise, is almost always from God.

7. *Satan and Religious Experiences*

A problem has been mentioned to me on enough occasions to see it as something that can happen even with the initial gift.

A very devout woman had been prayed over, had received the beginning gift, but came the next week with some religious problems she had never encountered before. The same thing happened to a priest in the middle of a retreat. All that can be said is that in being open to the Holy Spirit, the person also can open himself to problems with other spirits.

Sometimes, together with the initial religious experience, the person also has some unique experiences with a spirit of confusion, or spirit of depression, or of doubts against faith.

Usually a simple explanation and a prayer for the removal of the influence is enough to remedy the situation.

If, however, the person has been involved in occult powers, the initial religious experience will stir up some deeply rooted involvement that needs more help than just an explanation and prayer.

Therefore, even with the initial experience, there are sometimes aspects that need to be discerned.

11

Do Religious Experiences Remain?

"Lord how good that we are here! With your permission, I will erect three booths here, one for you, one for Moses and one for Elijah."

(Matt. 17:4)

Unfortunately, we priests have had a lot of spirituality that didn't work. For many priests, religious experiences are associated with "first fervor", those innocent, early days of seminary life.

A primary objection to everything in this book would be — "I tried them and they don't last" "They go away" "You can't live by emotion".

My message is "They are not supposed to go away. Religious experiences that go away are the seeds stolen by the birds of the air, or withered by the sun or strangled by the thorns."

Religious experiences aren't valued because so many priests have only a superficial acquaintance.

The priest would never claim there is nothing to French or Spanish, just because he never got into the language deeply. A stream isn't satisfying or powerful until we get deep enough to swim or be carried along.

Certainly, the power of religious experiences that never remained is little. But they are meant to remain, and only in remaining can God finish His work in us.

The following stories stress the permanency of the religious experience gift.

1. Only A Retreat Experience?

Every priest has been greeted by innumerable retreat masters with the words "Lord, it is good that we are here".

We usually felt pretty good, too – the burdens of work set aside, a few days of quiet, a chance to rest. But we were just as happy to return to that work.

Are religious experiences only novitiate experiences, retreat experiences, "from time to time" experiences? Are they rare experiences, passing experiences, possibly here today, certainly gone tomorrow experiences?

Are they experiences to get us priests out of a problem, or over an addiction? Are they special gifts when we have special problems? Or are they every day experiences?

For too long we have heard, "Lord, it is good to be here" and believed that religious experiences are a "retreat house only" gift.

2. The People's Stories

During the last few years, I have given many talks about religious experiences. Naturally, these talks are filled with stories. Afterwards people came up to tell me their story of their beginning religious experiences.

The people's stories always seemed to have the same elements – a searching, a reaching out to God, a religious experience and a gift of God's presence. Unfortunately, the stories ended there. The fleeting moments of religious experiences had passed away. Many didn't even realize what happened to them. Because they didn't understand, they also didn't talk about the gift or seek direction.

Religious experiences are not meant to be for one, shining moment like a Camelot. They are the seed cast on the ground that must find good soil to take root.

However, the people felt that no one would understand and no one could explain. Their priests didn't talk about religious experiences or meeting Jesus, so the seed died and brought forth no new life.

3. Solving A Problem

A priest had left the active ministry and had gotten himself deeply involved in an alcohol problem. Although a priest from the prayer group kept closely in touch, the case looked hopeless. From time to time, the priest would come and pray with us. He accepted in great faith the simplicity of the charismatic prayer groups and was frequently touched by God and often sought prayers for his well-being.

After a few years, God's gift of freedom from alcohol came. He saw clearly God's will and decided to enter a place of rehabilitation. The treatment was successful and for the last four years he has lived a sober life, now holding a very responsible job.

After his treatment, he returned to the priest prayer group, and over the next year came closer and closer to a return to active ministry. Since then he has not come back, and the question of a return has been put off even though he is more stable and has made no move in any other direction.

I can't claim to know God's will for him, but I think his case illustrates a truth, an extremely important truth — God is never finished acting through religious experiences.

Often priests with questions or problems come to the prayer group. They receive the spiritual help they need, but then don't continue.

That is a shame, because religious experiences aren't just "problem-solving" helps. There is the saying "Be patient, God isn't finished with me yet." However, if there is no regular gift of religious experiences you certainly aren't letting Him get on with the job.

4. The Projects Didn't Blossom

A priest once sat very skeptically at a talk I was asked to give on Charismatic Renewal. Strange thing, though — he found himself getting into his car the next week and driving to the prayer meeting.

He came with great enthusiasm and moved quickly into many works. Somewhere along the way, though, something happened. Some of his projects didn't blossom as he thought, so he decided that this phase of his priestly search for God was over.

Sometimes priests reach a certain level and are satisfied. They have their head above water, and feel that religious experiences have done their task, and that their time is over.

However, there is no such thing as a "time for religious experiences". Once begun, these experiences should never cease. Whatever changes occurred through the beginning experiences, are as nothing compared to what lies ahead.

God's work in us is always unfinished, and his power in these experiences is not meant to go away after some initial changes.

5. We Lost The Gift

One evening I had helped a married couple yield to the power of prayer tongues. This manifestation of the Spirit remains with the person permanently. However, a week later the couple came to me, worried because "we lost the gift". What existed was really just doubts and, with a little help, they yielded to the gift, never to lose it again.

A central question concerning religious experiences is whether the gift is ever lost. This book teaches that these experiences are *primary results of Baptism. Primary* means "early on" in the Christian life, easily available to beginners. *Results* means effects of the Holy Spirit's indwelling. *Of Baptism* means this gift is available to all the baptized.

However, religious experiences can easily be lost, and are often more difficult to regain than to receive for the first time.

If that is true, then why bother with these gifts at all? Why not stay with just the permanent gifts — such as sacraments, liturgy and formal prayers?

It is true that religious experiences are easily lost, often a problem, and always need careful watching. But the same objections are true of children! What the world would be like without children, so, the Church is like without religious experiences.

Praying in tongues is a gift that permanently remains with the priest. I wished the same could be true of religious experiences.

Part Four

Religious
Experiences
and Ministry

When I received my first assignment, my mother commented, "Well, you have no worries, you go right into an already established business." That was a good definition of the Catholic priest hood in 1962 — "an already established business."

But so much has changed, and just what constitutes priestly ministry these days is very much up for grabs. It is true that we have passed through the "crazy period" when the search for ministry involved just about anything. However, it is also true that no one has come up with any answers, and some don't even realize there are questions.

The following tries to state the problem:

1) The priesthood before the mid-1960's was a powerful institution.

2) This power was not political, but came from the important place the Church (and priesthood) had in the hearts and minds of the people.

3) This role is now diminished due to many factors, especially the vast number of varied experiences now available to the people.

4) This diminished role is perceived by the young, and results in fewer vocations.

5) This diminished role is perceived by priests and has been handled in various ways — e.g. leaving the priesthood, lowered expectations.

The most important and saddest point is that no powerful priesthood is emerging, and with fewer seminarians, the American priesthood might be inevitably locked into a much less powerful role for good.

Years ago there was an awareness of the poverty of Catholic liturgical music. After the criticism, some complained that the critics had taken away the old hymns and not supplied anything new. Now, however, a wealth of good hymns and creativity are present.

The same does not seem to be happening to priestly ministry. Much of the old has gone, but nothing has come forth to once more lift the Church and priesthood to a place of power.

From this point on, the book shifts from urging religious experiences for the priest's own good, to explaining the power these experiences can give to his ministry.

12

Jesus and Ministry

---

among whom are you who have been called to belong to Jesus Christ. (Romans 1:6)

I continually thank my God for you because of the favor he has bestowed on you in Christ Jesus.
(1 Cor 1:4)

he likewise predestined us through Christ Jesus to be his adopted sons. (Eph 1:5)

"Am I not free? Am I not an apostle? Have I not seen Jesus Our Lord? And are you not my work in the Lord?" (1 Cor 9:1)

The Church has taught us to end all prayers with "through Christ Our Lord", But where is Jesus in the priest's ministry? Is He far away, having long ago given a command to "go teach all nations" and then left to sit at the Father's right hand? Or is He the risen Jesus, still appearing and acting just when we need Him most?

To put the question another way — is Jesus someone you talk about to your parishioners, or is He a Person to whom you introduce your parishioners?

The question might seem too simple, but, the first, central and basic question of priestly ministry has to be "Where is Jesus Christ in the priest's ministry?". No powerful ministry begins until the priest answers that question.

The following stories try to help the priest see the importance of the question, "Where is Jesus in your ministry", because the priest can respond with the easy answers: "Sure, Jesus is there.", "Don't I believe in Jesus?" "Don't the people believe in Jesus?" "Jesus is everywhere in my ministry".

If Jesus is just "everywhere" in the priest's ministry, then He is really "nowhere". The only place and time Jesus manifests His power is in the concrete, individual situation.

The consecration at mass isn't "everywhere". It is at the altar and at a definite part of the liturgy. Jesus in our ministry isn't just everywhere. At definite times and places during the day, He comes in power.

The following stories face the question of presence of Jesus in ministry.

1. What Did I Bring?

Two religious experiences are landmarks in my priesthood — the 1954 gift of prayer and the 1971 gift, which I call my "gift of ministry".

Concerning the nine years of priesthood that preceded the second gift, I have often reflected, "Just what did I bring to the people from ordination day 1962 to the 1971 ministry experience?"

My 1962 priesthood was rooted in prayer, and God's presence remained with me. Yet, I didn't bring God to the people. I brought a God-touched me. That was the best I could do in those days.

It could be described as this —

Each day I went before God and experienced Him very deeply. I then went out to His people, in the most intelligent, orderly out-reaching way I could conceive. Results occurred. People returned to Church. The confessional lines were long ones. The office calls were many. I believed, then and now, that God was using me. But I still believe that they were getting "me touched by God" and not the Lord Himself.

The 1971 experience changed that — not that the "intelligent orderly, out-reaching ways of ministry" ceased, but now the people were not getting "me touched by God". They began to receive God and His power.

In June 1971, about a month after the second religious experience, I spoke at a Catholic girls high school. I had been there often, offering to them stories and the best preaching I could muster. The effects were good enough that I kept being asked back.

After the mass and homily, a religious sister, not knowing anything of what had happened, came over and said, "Father, you are different. Something happened because there is a new simplicity in your preaching."

What was different? I no longer tried to lead the girls to God through me. I knew now that everyone could directly know the Lord. As the Samaritans said to the woman at the well,

> *"No longer does our faith depend on your story. We have heard for ourselves, and we know that this is really the Savior of the world."*   (Jn 4:42)

2. See You Next Saturday

Yesterday as I was walking by a football field, a group aged 25 to 35 began to clap for me. I soon found out why — they needed another player to even up the sides. After a half hour, when somebody else came along, I left the group, being greeted with "See you next Saturday, Father".

It was a good feeling to be accepted by that age group and to be known as a priest. As I was walking home, however, I reflected that my goal of ministry was changed now. No longer do I seek that people come to know me, the priest, the Church representative, but to know Jesus. That is a whole new step — both for the people and for me.

In the early years of ministry, I never dreamed of that goal. I ran around the parish, sometimes very effectively, rounding up people who would receive Sacraments because they knew me, or because I helped them.

My eyes are now opened. Everyone, by faith and Baptism, has the power to know Jesus Christ — to meet Him in a personal, saving way and to have that initial meeting continue into a full life in Christ.

As I walked home I felt good about two things — the warm reception by the young men, but especially that my ministry was no longer limited to getting people to know me. Ministry now has a whole different power than it used to.

3. Will Your Work Last?

One day in a psychology seminar this tremendous priest professor asked, "How can you tell if someone has a vocation?" After our stupid answers, he said, "You look inside and you see what is there. Can't you look inside a seed, and tell what it would be if you planted it? Then why can't you look inside people and know what they will become if they get planted right?"

For us priests, the same reply can be given to our ministry. What kind of priesthood will we have? Well just look. Look inside yourself and what do you see? Do you see God there? Do you see religious experiences? Do you see Jesus Christ? Do you see the gifts of the Spirit?

If you find only human talents, and human goals, and human strivings then you will have a human priesthood and much of your work will not stand the test of the Day of the Lord.

While writing this section, I happened to be listening to the New Testament on cassettes. The following lines struck me on this point:

> The Day will disclose it. That day will make its appearance with fire; and the fire will test the quality of each man's work. If the building a man has raised on this foundation still stands, he will receive his recompense: if a man's building burns, he will suffer loss. He himself will be saved but only as one fleeing through fire.   (1 Cor 3:13-15)

4. Preaching Jesus

I always enjoyed preaching. Writing comes easily and my memory could string together a host of stories. But all of that is changed. The stories are different now. They are stories of what Jesus has done, so everyone realizes that Jesus is near.

The power in preaching comes from Jesus. Just at the liturgy has special moments when God acts (the Consecration or Communion), so preaching in the Lord has special moments —

Enough.

---

moments when God touches preacher and listener and both are led beyond the words to Jesus.

For this to happen, a few conditions are needed:

1) The preacher must experience the power of Jesus acting upon his own infirmities and needs.
2) He preaches, then, a Jesus who cares and who will intervene.
3) The preacher doesn't speak *about* the biblical activity of God, but expects that biblical activity to happen in the liturgy.
4) The preacher is convinced that every person in the congregation needs Jesus, and they will experience some action, some moment of Jesus within them.

"The moment your greeting sounded in my ears,
the baby leapt in my womb for joy." (Luke 1:44)

In this preaching, the priest is helpless because he looks for some divine action to bless and complete his human words. The helplessness is not that of an unprepared preacher. The helplessness lies in what the priest seeks for the people — the gift that Jesus wants to bestow at that moment.

5. A Church Filled With Experiences

On a couple of occasions now, Americans have faced gasoline crises — long lines at the gas station and the lifestyle changes that must occur when that energy is not available. The crises were shortlived, seemingly brought about to get price rises.

The "crises" were terminated when American motorists got angry with the oil companies. One thing was sure — motorists knew the importance of cars being filled with gasoline.

Unfortunately, we priests do not know the value of Church life filled with religious experiences. The early Church knew it. However, after the first century, universal religious experiences were not the ordinary Church life. So, we priests grew up in a Church which just accepted people not having an experience of Jesus Christ.

In our day, "born again" Churches make the beginning religious experience an absolute requirement, preaching that everyone is to be born again. That religious experience tide continues to grow. We priests can look askance at their theology, and see how they misinterpret Scripture. Yet these Churches have captured some piece of the original Church life, where Baptism was a life-changing event, an immersion, a powerful transfer from the Kingdom of darkness to the Kingdom of light.

Especially, priests in America cannot say that expecting everyone in the parish to have the gift of religious experiences is unreal, when all around us the "born again" Churches strive to do just that.

6. A File Filled With Suffering

A psychiatrist wanted to write a book on inner healing. However, as he went to his file to recall concrete cases, he was overwhelmed by the amount of suffering contained in that single cabinet.

In my first year as a priest, on our annual house to house visitation, a number of people shared with me their marriage problems. I still remember standing there in the street, looking at the long row of houses and being overwhelmed with the amount of suffering taking place within them.

How, as priests, do we handle that reality in our parish? It's everywhere in overwhelming amounts. We have three options – we can run liturgies, as if everyone who enters our Church brings no burdens, or we can jump into the problems with all our human counseling skills (and be quickly wiped out).

Or we can enter into the mystery of Jesus – who neither removed Himself from human suffering, nor was overcome by it; nor allowed Himself to respond with merely human answers.

There are "answers" and "solutions" to human suffering, but they are contained in no psychology book (although that can help). The answer and solution to every problem of human suffering is in the Father's mind. No one answer exists. No preconceived solution. So, if the priest is to help at all in the mystery of human suffering, he has to be able to enter the Father's mind. The only door is Jesus, and the only entrance is by religious experiences.

"Father, Lord of heaven and earth, to you I offer praise; for what you have hidden from the learned and the clever you have revealed to the merest children."

(Matt 11:25)

13

Searching For Ministry

A door has been opened wide for my work. . .
(1 Cor 16:9)

If the ministry of death, carved in writing on stone, was inaugurated with such glory that the Israelites could not look on Moses' face because of the glory that shone on it (even though it was a fading glory), how much greater will be the glory of the ministry of the Spirit?
(2 Cor 3:7-8)

In the late sixties, a stress was placed on "doing your own thing". Unfortunately, the "do your own thing" ministry of the sixties was often built upon the swirling sand of the priest's own feelings, the latest idea of "meaningful" ministry, or goals, taken from political movements.

However, the "do your own thing" ministry, as all such movements had within it a grain of truth – the need for each priest to search. Unfortunately the search centered on the priest, and often on his own emotional needs.

In the Catholic theology of priesthood, there is a "do your own thing" piece – the mystery of God's intention in calling a young man to ordination. No priest should set that piece aside and just "function" or be an "ecclesiastic".

Inevitably, the whole "do your thing" ministry went down the tube and the Church has now withdrawn again to a sacramental approach (which is a lot safer), that is somewhat "enlightened" by the understanding of Scriptural Renewal, the use of psychological insights, and a liturgical focus.

But neither "do your own thing", nor an "enlightened sacramental approach" is enough. Each priest's ministry is a mystery of God's call and demands that the priest be searching and looking.

The following stories delve into the question of a priest searching for his ministry.

1. Two Classes Of Priests

An obedience exists in the priesthood that should never be destroyed. After due consultation, the priest receives a letter or a phone call telling him to go to an assignment and he goes. However with the "obedience approach" the priest can adopt the attitude that "doing what he is told" is all he needs to do – that he exhausts God's Will by conforming to outside commands.

Searching for ministry always involves doors being opened. Sometimes the door is central, determining the priest's whole life. Sometimes the door is so large that many others can enter, as with religious communities. But to have a door open, demands a priest who is searching. Some priests seem aware of this process. Other priests seem totally oblivious to both the gift of personal religious experiences and the need to search for a ministry.

A question has to be seriously raised, "Are there two classes of priests?" – those whom God has called to search and those called merely to function? Put another way – is every priest meant to experience God, and because of that experience to have a God given ministry?

The easier answer could be to claim that not every priest is called to a "God given ministry" – that many are just meant to function in Church. It is easier to say that religious experiences and charisms are for the few.

I believe that a "God-given ministry" is for every priest. The reality will come faster than we dream, if we are willing to go beyond the routine duties bestowed by obedience and begin to search.

2. To Live Again

About eight years ago, a woman walked into a rectory with a complaint against the Church. She had just lost her husband, and could find no one – in the Church or outside the Church – to help her with her grief. The priest who answered that rectory doorbell was just a resident in the parish, being assigned full time as principal to the nearby Catholic high school.

However, he listened to the woman and then made phone calls to what he considered the proper Church offices for help.

He realized that these offices really offered no help in this area. Instead of just turning the woman away, he felt called by God to be of help.

Two things happened. First, he discovered that even though the parish was basically young, there were a number of recent widows. Secondly, he began to get out books on the question of the "grief cycle", gradually understanding the ten stages that people go through after the death of a spouse. As he gathered the widows, they reviewed these books and formed an organization called To Live Again (TLA), that has helped many widows and widowers to go through the grief cycle and (in some instances) to find a good future partner.

Every priest is not called to begin an organization. The lesson, however, is important. There are moments when God is trying to open a door. The door can be anything – someone with a need, or a personal experience, or an idea from God. The priest needs the sensitivity that comes from experiencing God's touch within himself, to recognize God's call at that moment.

3. A Spanish Apostolate

By 1955, the previous year's gift of religious experience had brought forth a desire to serve. The seeking for ministry was all mixed up, but the yearning was there. Finally, my pastor directed me to Spanish apostolate and that resulted in six summers of pre-ordination ministry. That time was important in answering my own vocational question and later opened very important doors of ministry.

The story has an important teaching – religious experiences must result in a desire to serve. The priest won't know exactly how, or even where, but eventually God will open the right door.

4. Things Shifting Around

A priest friend of mine always talked about the ecology of change – that whenever a change is introduced, other aspects down the road and totally forgotten about, will be caught up in that change.

The many crises of the 70's and 80's have caused worldwide changes. Future crises and inventions will continue the rapid pace of a constantly changing world.

So the priesthood is in a whirlpool of change, not so much from within as from without.

To what does the modern priest cling for his identity — to his task; his theology; his special skill; his institutional Church?

During my seminary years, books on priesthood abounded — models of how to be good priest. Both the books and the models remained quite constant during those years. Now, everything constantly changes.

A priest can refuse to change, claiming that the pendulum will inevitably swing back. Or, he can change with every wind.

In the shifting sand of the modern world, the priest should be doing two things:

1) Be experiencing Jesus Christ who *"is the same yesterday, today and forever"* (Heb 13:8)

2) Be searching for the doors that God will open.

5. *Doors Not Ideas*

Many times in ministry I have had excellent ideas. Most of them totally failed. The others brought forth little fruit after much effort. The most fruitful ministry didn't come from ideas but doors that opened suddenly.

Priests have excellent ideas but ideas don't build the kingdom. Frequently they are blocks to God's actions. These ideas lead a priest to all kinds of works, many hours sacrificed for people, and more miles put on the car. The results are small. The priest either grows discouraged or increases his daily pace.

Instead, the priest should allow God to take away the ideas (often the ones he most cherishes and feels are most central to his priesthood) and open to him the true doors of ministry.

These doors are God's idea for his priesthood. It's obviously impossible to have God's ideas without religious experiences. If the priest cannot listen to God, the best he can do is just run around in the light of his own ideas.

6. *One Person's Need*

I once came across a family in the parish who had a young son, eleven years old, who had not as yet made his First Communion. The mother was interested, but didn't want the child to attend classes with six and seven year olds. That night a young college girl volunteered to teach the child.

Eventually, I realized there were a large number of children in similar circumstances, and soon about thirty were receiving these types of instructions. Both teacher and the pupil enjoyed the experience.

Priests aren't meant just to bounce from appointment to appointment, nor just to fulfill specified parochial goals. They are meant to experience God's call. The call is God's mystery, often manifested to the priest in some person's need. In that need, a new door of ministry opens.

7. *Let The University Tell You*

Years ago I attended a three-day seminar on ministry to medical schools. It was a confusing three days, because no one had a clear idea of their identity. After about a day and a half, the whole conference broke down, so we were asked to break into small groups.

As our group gathered, another priest (there were about six of us at this conference) said that we should talk about our identity and what role we bring to the University. The moderator responded with the ultimate statement of confusion, "We should not tell the university what role we have. We should ask the university what role they want us to have." Translated that meant that if the university wanted the chaplain to handle curriculum, or to run group therapy sessions, or to make social relationships easier, then that was supposed to be the chaplain's role.

Chaplaincies, especially at medical universities, are frontier apostolates. The question, though, is valid for every type of priesthood. Where does the priest get his idea of ministry? There are many sources — from his theology of priesthood, from Church, from canon law, from the needs of the people, from the parish expectations, and from his brother priests.

All of the above are inadequate, for all are external to that mysterious relationship of God to His priest. No one called him to priesthood except God – not the Church, not his brother priests, not the people. The priest will never understand who he is or what he is called to, unless he experiences God.

14

Religious Experiences and Identity

The Lord has sworn, and he will not repent:
"You are a priest forever, according to the order
of Melchizedek." (Ps. 110)

But Moses said to God, "Who am I that I should go
to Pharoah and lead the Israelites out of Egypt?"
(Exodus 3:11)

Then King David went in and sat before the Lord
and said "Who am I, Lord God, and who are the
members of my house, that you have brought me
to this point?" (2 Sam 7:18)

Who Am I?

Who am I? From birth to death, that question is there. From another I was born. By others, I am given a name. Through others I learn a language, gain a culture and assume a role.

However, only by God is a person called to priesthood. To answer the question, "Who am I in the priesthood" requires a God experience. Anything else falls short. Without religious experiences I will never become the priest I'm meant to be.

The following stories outline the failure of any other method of finding the priestly identity.

1. You're Not Going To Last

About five years ago, I had an enjoyable dinner with a priest with a graduate degree. The conversation was lively and the priest had a lot of insights into people. As we sat there, toward the end of the evening, I said to him what I have never said to any other priest. "You won't last long in the priesthood". He asked me why. I had to say that it was because I found he had a lot of human insights but he seemed to possess no spiritual gifts. There were many human experiences but there were no religious experiences. The statement wasn't made to get him to leave, but just to warn him what ultimately would occur.

Many priests remain in priesthood without religious experiences, but this priest was different. He had an excellent mind, a specialized training, and he would logically come to the question of why he should be a priest, when all he was doing was offering human help. He asked that question six months later, and answered it by leaving.

The central question, asked often in seminary years and the early years of priesthood is "Why should I be a priest?" Obviously today many young men can't get that question answered, so they don't even enter the seminary. For others, the question is often pushed into the background as they "adjust" to the seminary and to priesthood.

But the question is important. It shouldn't torment a priest, but it shouldn't be set aside. The question should be answered.

Because the Lord is our portion, a priest has to be experiencing God to be able to answer that question, for himself and for his people.

2. What's Happening Within?

It was 1970 and the American Bishops had just issued their guidelines concerning mixed marriages. I was discussing these guidelines with a couple of other priest canon lawyers. One was greatly upset. He saw the whole document as destructive and pulling down essential parts of Church life. After the discussion, we went to lunch. I still remember walking along with that priest, realizing that he had no inner identity. His whole priesthood was external, and changes in the law threatened his whole world.

A few months later the priest came to tell me he was leaving; that there had been many times, even before ordination, when he wondered about his vocation. There had been different moments, and different events, that had called him back, but now there was just nothing that could hold him.

Because of the previous conversation months earlier, the problem was a clear one. There was just nothing inside. Very possibly, through no fault of his own, priesthood was just a shell that had fallen apart.

There is no way, in one easy answer, to handle the question of a vocational collapse. Yet a few points could be made:

1) The most important part of a vocation is what is going on within – the feelings, hopes, understandings, the gradual putting things together, so that the vocation is built upon the rock.

2) The most important part of what is happening within is what is going on between the priest and his God.

When a vocation collapses, when a priest feels he is at the end of his rope, someone or some group has to take time to help the priest sort through the rubble to find if any little flame still exists.

Although this process must occur on many levels, restoration to the priesthood happens most effectively when the priest sees clearly that the core of priesthood is an inner relationship to God.

3. The Unasked Question

A young priest from another diocese came about six months ago. He was totally confused, manifesting some psychosomatic physical problems, and wondering about his priesthood. He felt he had a lot of questions and wondered if he could answer them in the active ministry. His identity problem was a fairly common question. For many priests, the question is buried; for many others it has long ago been set aside; for others, even to ask the question, seems hopeless.

The problem comes forth in many ways — depression, searching, chronic fatigue, a sense of "being locked in", a lowering of expectation and sometimes a "private life".

The identity question is a complex one and I would not teach that a priest just has to experience God to suddenly "find himself".

I would teach that:

1) Religious experiences clear up many fuzzy areas.
2) They help the priest see the importance of the spiritual dimensions of life.
3) They force the priest to face his identity problems.
4) They have helped a number of priests return to the active ministry.
5) They safeguard the gift of a vocation, if it is truly there.

Religious experiences are the good soil of the vocational seed. In their absence, where does the seed root itself?

4. Saying "No"

Recently I was asked to go to Miami for a priest retreat. A few weeks later a request came from St. Petersburg. To a Philadelphian, nothing looks better than a few winter weeks in the Florida sun. Having prayed over the requests, I turned them down and provided other priests from the prayer group as retreat masters.

All of the above represents a real shift in decision making. In the early years of priesthood, every request was seen like the seminary bell — the Vox Dei. In those early years, everyone was given time freely.

The change is not due just to growing up in the priesthood, or even just to growing older and slowing down. The change results from a clearer idea of God.

A priest's identity should not come primarily through the claims people make upon him. If they do, then little by little he loses his identity — even the identity God seeks for him.

Through religious experiences, the priest should know his call. He should have entered God's mind and had answered, in some fashion, the question, "Why did you call me to be a priest?"

To be sent on an active ministry with no personal idea of God's call is devastating and fruitless. The disciples knew they were to heal, to cast out demons and to proclaim that the Kingdom of heaven was at hand. If people asked them to do something else, they knew they weren't sent for that reason.

A priest can get into endless tasks to which he is not even called by God. If he hasn't discerned his call, he will let people waste his time. He then complains that there is so little fruit from all his many works. A priest truly seeking God's work, should first experience God and learn what works God wants him to do.

5. *No Longer Defined By Theology*

In 1965, at a coffee shop in Rome, I met some seminarians from the Spanish College. They asked me when I was ordained, and when I said 1962, they looked at me, smiled and said "Oh, preconciliar". Suddenly, my three year old priesthood was outmoded!

That preconciliar theology, together with the parochialism that could flourish before television devasted the family, provided the priest with his identity. That identity gave thousands of priests a personality security that none of us can claim today.

To refresh your memory — that preconciliar theology stressed the state of grace, the priest's power to forgive sins, divine guidance of the Church so that "what the Church said" was equated with God's mind; the priest's power over the Eucharist; the need for the priest at the death bed; the unique nature of the Catholic Church and the clear benefits derived from being a member of the true Church.

That theology's power over people's lives no longer exists; and a priest who sees his role as reinforcing or reintroducing that theology is involved in a hopeless task. The world has changed too much.

The problem is, where, then, does the priest get his identity? The priest ordained in the 1940's through early 1960's had a clear theological identity, that found a lived reality in the average parish (that is, the people through the Baltimore Catechism shared the same theology). Priests ordained after that have another theological identity. Both sets of priests find the lived reality of the parish a very confused theology (that is, the people at this point think in all kinds of ways).

This theological babel is a problem. It's also God's invitiation to rediscover the central Christian experience — Jesus Christ.

If the sheep are scattered theologically, the answer rests in the priest coming to know the Good Shepherd. The sheep always hear His voice.

6. *Functioning Without A Structure*

A recent trip took another priest and myself into many diocesan office buildings. We began to comment how all the buildings seemed the same and how going into a diocesan office building wasn't much different than going into a secular office building where the company made soap or televisions or cars.

The same can be said of priests. Our tasks are similar to secular fields, usually Administration, or teaching. Even "running a parish" can be done like "running a store."

The point is this — the Church has tasks to get done, and, since priests are full time, these tasks fall to us. Yet as we look at what we do, we honestly have to admit that "getting the tasks done" doesn't require a lot of faith.

Often the tasks can keep the priest from asking himself just what he does believe. They can actually isolate the priest from God.

The question can be put this way — what if tomorrow we were stripped of our usually priestly "tasks," of going into a building or teaching in a school, or running a parish, would we know where to begin?

What would the priest do if he were back at the first Pentecost and had only the religious experiences of the Easter visions and the Pentecostal outpouring of the Spirit? Could he function only with the enthusiasm of the Early Church? With no structure? With no defined tasks? With just his experience of Jesus and the power of the Spirit?

Part Five

Religious
Experiences
and Power

During the first nine years of priesthood, my ministry was filled with life-changing events. These changes occurred because the people in the early 1960's still gave the priest a special role, and sought his help in life's important decisions.

During these years, my ministry was a combination of extreme availability, sensitivity, the cultural role given to priests, a zeal nourished by prayer, clear church teaching and God's power. Looking at the above, it would be hard to say what was missing.

Yet beginning in 1970, a feeling grew within me that my ministry was not effective. In fact, looking over the pastoral scene, I didn't see anyone's ministry really being that effective. There were not the significant changes in people's lives in the early 1970's that I had seen in the early 1960's.

At thirty-five years of age, my priesthood had, for one terrible moment, come up against a wall, a dead end. The day was April 4th, 1971, a Saturday afternoon set aside for ministry to the student doctors at Jefferson Hospital. These Saturday afternoons usually consisted of knocking on doors, sitting in apartments and seeing how I could help the student doctors in their Catholic faith.

On April 4th, the feelings of a fruitless ministry were growing within. As I drove the few miles to downtown Philadelphia, these feelings overwhelmed me. Instead of parking my car, I drove past the lot, turned around and went home.

On Sunday, April 5th, my sister-in-law began to speak to me about her prayer group participation, and especially about the important changes it had made in her life.

I was suddenly transported back nine years – to a church that was able to bring about life-changing effects. In that moment, all the lights went on and there began the second spring of my priesthood – a God given ministry immersed in the powers of the Spirit.

The following chapters attempt to share the treasury of God's powers that have been opened to me since April 1971.

15

Power In Ministry

With power the Apostles bore witness to the Resurrection of the Lord Jesus, . . .   (Acts 4:33)

I am not ashamed of the gospel. It is the power of God leading everyone who believes in it to salvation, the Jew first, then the Greek. (Romans 1:16)

. . .by those who preach the gospel to you in the power of the Holy Spirit sent from heaven.

(1 Peter 1:12)

I opened the paper yesterday and read of:

1) The new drug, Interferon, to cure cancer.
2) Plans to build a supercomputer.
3) Growing influence of organized crime.
4) Latest advances in television technology.

The modern world is filled with power — good, bad, indifferent. The priesthood is getting swallowed up by the power of other phases of human life.

We priests shy away from power. It connotes to us Church politics, or manipulation of people. Even our work for people, we tend to think of "system" more than "power". We have the parish, the school system, and the sacramental system.

All of these systems are becoming powerless. They still exist. People still come to Church, attend our schools, and receive the sacraments. These same people, however, are also swept up in the new powers of the modern world.

So, it's time to ask the question, "Where is our power?" Our power is in the resurrection of Jesus and the Holy Spirit.

The following stories don't deal with the liturgy, the school or the sacraments. All of those should remain with us. Besides our "system", we priests have to seek God's power.

1. A Japanese Addict

About five years ago, a Maryknoll missionary came to our prayer group. After the prayer meeting, I usually spent time with my leaders. This night, I knew the usual routine had to be changed for this priest. Since then I have met him about four times, whenever he returns home from Japan.

Last Christmas, he told me the beginning of a powerful story and just yesterday, his Christmas greeting brought me up to date. A Japanese man was an alcoholic. Besides that he had an accident that caused both lower limbs to be amputated. As if those problems weren't enough, the man became addicted to drugs while in the hospital. With all these problems he had contracted large debts.

At this point, the priest was led to take the man into his house. The man had no religious background and didn't even believe in God. After a few weeks, the priest asked the man to say a fifteen second prayer each day. God's power began. In a few weeks, it was obvious that God was freeing the man from his addictions. He is now totally cured, is employed in rehabilitation programs and has all the zeal of the most fervent missionary in going out to other addicts.

Two points, extremely clear in this case, are really true of every person we priests meet:

1) Whether the person has a small problem, or seemingly insurmountable, multiple problems, we are powerless to help them if we use only human means.
2) Any problem can be solved by God.

These two truths are simple, yet it is difficult to live always in the clarity of those beliefs, not thinking that our own power is sufficient and never despairing of God's power.

If the priest had only offered the man the human help (extraordinary as it was), he would today still be a helpless addict.

2. A Sick Child

One evening, a religious sister called, prompted by that day's gospel of the Centurion, asking if I would pray for a fifth grader who had been taken quickly from school for surgery. The operation had been performed that day and involved replacing some shunts to the child's head. The sister wasn't asking me to go, since it was late at night and the hospital was in the inner city.

After talking to her, I telephoned the hospital. The voice on the other end said I would be more than welcome even at that hour.

When I went, the child was asleep but seemingly in great distress. I decided to anoint him because the sacrament had not been given in the rush to operate. As soon as the anointing was finished, he opened his eyes and, as if he had been awake all along, said clearly, "Thank you, Father." I talked with him a little about his school and the sister who asked me to pray.

Then the child realized he was in pain and began to call out for his mother. I felt perplexed since the child's second state seemed worse than the first, yet there had already been signs of God acting. All I could do was to pray over the child. In ten seconds he was asleep, this time into a deep and sound sleep.

Certainly, I do not claim any great gift of healing, but now I go to hospitals in quite a different frame of mind. Formerly the time and inconvenience involved seemed so out of proportion to the amount of consolation given to the sick person.

Now, however, I go in a different Spirit. The going has a mystery and a power that comes from a very simple and child-like faith in Jesus. I do not bring the sick my presence, or even my great words of sympathy. Instead I bring the power and the love of Jesus Christ.

3. A Rock Group

In late 1976 we visited the Spectrum (the Philadelphia version of Madison Square Garden) to prepare for our New Year's Day prayer meeting and mass to be held there.

That evening the rock group "Kiss" was going to perform (to its usual sell-out crowd.) Just as we left, the group got up to practice. With the overwhelming microphone the gripping power of that music overflowed the building. It was a total experience and I could only imagine what a complete immersion into that power would take place that night in the sold-out teenage crowd.

As we went outside into the bitter December weather, it was six hours before the doors opened. The wind-chill factor was so low that the five minutes getting to the car was difficult. Yet, a boy and a girl wrapped in a blanket were standing there waiting to be first in line at the ticket window.

We have tough competition for the minds and hearts of the young. If a scorecard were accurately kept, I think we would be losing. Possibly many will cite the passing of the Vietnam troubles and return to conservatism, as signs of a return to "normalcy" among the young. But that is really naive.

The central question is "power". Who has power to gain their commitment? It is wrong for the Church to trust in sociological factors over which it has little control. The Church has to look within itself and and see what powers Jesus provides.

4. Prayers In The Barber Shop

I have just come back from the barber shop. The shop is filled with faith. Immediately before the owner's death, six months ago from cancer, I dedicated "Lead My People" to him and his family.

I would always repay him for his haircut by praying over him, right there in front of all his customers. As time went on, I ended up praying over the four others who worked for him. To this day the four still have me pray over them each time. Today, as I entered, the one worker mentioned how much the prayer had meant to him.

In the early years of priesthood, my ministry had only two such moments of praying over people — the short formal blessing a priest gives when leaving the house, and the formal act of absolution. This is still a powerful moment for me, and remains the most powerful laying on of hands.

But much more frequent is the informal laying on of hands. It is impossible to hear confessions in the barber shop, but it is very easy to impose hands and pray. Often there are tears, or a feeling of relief. I can say clearly — my priesthood is much more powerful and much more effective, because of the ministry of laying on of hands.

Seven times the New Testament mentions these rites of laying on of hands. Unfortunately, our theology got caught up in proving various sacraments through these rites. When I was ordained, no one had even told me just to lay hands and pray for God's power.

So I visited homes, counselled, gave advice (some good, some bad), took office calls, consoled, met people on a meaningful level, quoted the latest theology and hundreds of other things — but I never laid hands and prayed that the power of Jesus Christ would change these people or help their problems.

Now, I never hesitate to lay hands. Something always happens — healing, understanding, patience, discernment of God's will — something the person needed and would never have received without the laying on of hands.

5. Faith and Crowds

I was involved once, with a priest who has a large weekly healing ministry as well as an expanding radio program. He has two basic insights into ministry, both of which centered upon himself, but it was a centering coming from faith.

The first theory deals with faith, and the way God will use the priest.

One time, a woman came to him, who wasn't sure she believed in God. However, she said to him, "I believe in you". Most priests would have backed away or grown pompous. Instead, he said to her — Well, that's enough faith, now let us pray."

His second theory has to do with crowds. This priest loves the crowds and delights in them. He said to me "Crowds are a sign of God's blessing on the work. Never be afraid of the crowd. The people seem to be the first ones to sense where God is working".

There are too many faceless priests — priests whose names mean nothing and have no power to draw crowds. The Lord wants to change that. The crowds loved David, causing Saul's jealousy. The crowds loved Jesus. The real attraction is God — because the people quickly sense where they can find God's action in a human being. Every priest is meant to be in the middle of a crowd who see God's power in his ministry.

6. *I'll Go To The Doctor*

Five years ago, I was assigned to a parish where I had lived eight years before. The two elderly Irish ladies were still the housekeepers. One, however, was having a problem. As she brought in the food, the plate and cup and saucer would rattle. Dishes were sometimes dropped. I mentioned to the pastor her need for professional care. However, she would not go.

Each night, as I went down to get a glass of milk, Mary would be locking up before going to her room. She would agree to sit down for a few minutes to pray. She seemed to enjoy that and felt comfortable.

Every morning, Mary would walk over with me for the morning mass. One day the gospel contained healing stories, and in the homily I happened to mention that God's love for us in healing comes also through doctors, and we should take advantage of professional care. I completely forgot that Mary was listening until after it was said.

After mass, as I knelt in the Church, Mary walked up the aisle, stopped at my pew and said, "Father, I'll go to the doctor."

God's power had intervened in three steps:

1) The human advice that she needed help.
2) The simplicity of prayer together each night.
3) The gift of anointed preaching.

So, sometimes God's power comes quickly and suddenly, and sometimes the moment of breakthrough is preceded by other steps. Each case differs and the priest isn't limited to just one style of ministry, or a single method of approach. What is important, is that he realizes that situations will be straightened out only by God's power. The human level of caring and help is only the first step.

7. *And The Word Was Made Flesh*

Once when a priest discovered that a girl was thinking of an abortion, he asked the girl and her mother to come to the rectory. There he tried to convince both of them not to go through with the operation. Nothing worked.

Finally, the priest asked them to pray. As they did, he was led to read the opening of John's Gospel. When he finished the phrase "And the Word was made flesh and dwelt among us", both mother and daughter responded spontaneously, "There will be no abortion."

That story was told to me by the priest himself. It's a story I tend to recall when I, too, am immersed in what seems to be a pastoral dead-end; when no one is going to change. Not that I automatically get out John's Gospel, but I seek from God what to say or what to do. When human power is ended, divine power takes over. So when we priests have done everything possible in a pastoral situation, and things are falling apart, we shouldn't lose hope. Seek God's direction so His power enters the situation.

8. *Two Audiences*

By circumstances, I happened to be giving two talks to rather large groups a few days apart.

The first group were professional religious educators and the second group were primarily lay people involved in Charismatic Renewal. Their level of belief differed greatly.

For both groups, I worked hard and was basically happy with the prepared texts. When I stood before the religious educators, I felt no extra power. I gave the prepared text as well as I could — but that was all I gave. There were no high points, nothing extemporaneous, nothing that I really felt touched anyone. When that happens, I sometimes realize it's my own fault (too tired, not enough preparation or prayer). This time I knew it wasn't my fault. The problem was in the listeners. I experienced no living faith there. The group was not stirring me to reach in and feed them God's word. They weren't hungry. They were there for a professional convention — the annual one.

A few days later, there was a different talk to a deeply believing group. Everything was different. The prepared talk was only the starting place. (The talk never got finished.) The people were alive and God's power was touching many.

The different results were due not to me, nor to the prepared talk, but to the different levels of belief. The group without living faith got only the prepared talk. The group with living faith had the talk as a starting point, but got much, much more.

Recent years have seen a great renewal in preaching, but I've never seen any writing on the importance of the congregation's faith. Even with Jesus, the people's faith seemed to make Him go beyond what He intended to do.

Preaching will never be renewed by just changing the preacher. The congregation has to come prepared too!

9. God's Power In His People

One time in Mobile, the older waitresses took great delight in telling us priests about the great Sunday preaching they used to listen to for hours on end. After the meal, the other priests commented that the stories were from a different era.

Well, the congregations sitting in front of us priests are from a different era than thirty years ago. Their weekly lives are filled with innumerable experiences, practically all of them inimical to belief.

Do we priests realize that everything is different? Are we content that people just listen quietly while we preach? Do we understand the importance of religious experiences — our own and the people's — in preaching?

It's a different era, and if we don't seek God's power in our preaching, we are working on shifting sand.

16

Power Of Intercession

... but Jesus, because he remains forever, has a priesthood that does not pass away. Therefore he is always able to save those who approach God through him, since he forever lives to make intercession for them.   (Heb 7:25)

Simon's mother-in-law was in the grip of a severe fever, and they interceded with him for her.
                    (Luke 4:38)

A special chapter is devoted to intercession because every work of ministry should be rooted in this prayer.

Religious experiences unveil some basic truths:

1) The priest's own helplessness.
2) God's intense nearness.
3) The power and presence of the Kingdom.

The priest's message should be that "The Kingdom is at hand." He preaches, celebrates liturgy, plans, counsels, — all so the Kingdom can come in power.

But the priest is powerless to bring the Kingdom, which can only come from God.

Currently, we are preparing for three weekend Fall Conferences. Already this year, eight other events have happened. All eleven of these events are proceded by definite prayers of daily intercession by everyone involved.

We intercede before an event, so people will be touched by God to come. We intercede during the event, so nothing goes wrong and the people can experience God. We intercede after an event, so the people are faithful to the grace received at the event. So before and after every event large or small, we intercede.

The following are stories of that intercession, opening to you the treasure we have found.

1. Interceding on Vacation

One Thursday night on vacation, because the other priests would be gathering for the prayer meeting, I spent an hour of intercession for priests.

Next day, two startling events occurred both concerning priests. At breakfast, a woman knocked at the door, carrying a note from a priest that demanded an immediate reply. That afternoon another person brought a letter from yet another priest, speaking of his possible return to active ministry. In all my weeks of vacation, these are the only two letters I even remember receiving.

Frequently, God will call a priest to mind, and I will be led to pray for him. Sure enough, a few days later the priest will be calling.

Intercession permeates everything – before, during and afterward. This prayer represent our helplessness to bring about the Kingdom, yet our hope that the Kingdom's own power will come.

2. Going But Not Interceding

One night, on my way to give a talk, my mind wandered over a lot of issues and possible questions that might have to be handled. In coming near to the Church, I realized that I hadn't interceded for the evening. I hadn't asked God's blessing or invoked God's power. All I could think was "I'm going about this the same way I did before getting involved in this Renewal."

That was true. Before Charismatic Renewal, there were many invitations, many talks, and many nights driving to various parishes. However, there was no thought of intercession.

Intercession is not just a gimmick, not just a pious practice. Intercession proceeds every Conference, every event, every talk, even every counseling situation.

By intercession, the priest openly confesses that he has no power to touch people's hearts; that he does not even know what they need. However, he knows that God has given him a work and God's power will be there.

Two things are important:

1) Every invitation is discerned to see if God is calling to some work.
2) Every accepted invitation is surrounded by intercessory prayer.

That is quite a different ministry than taking every possible invitation and then arriving without a thought of intercession.

3. At A Sisters' Retreat

On a large sisters' retreat, the participants were asked to spend the evening praying for their communities. They were also told to return to their community and inform their Superior General that they had done this. After hearing about this intercession one Superior General told the sisters that that very evening she had five important decisions to make, and suddenly the answers had come clearly.

The story is a frequent one in the world of intercessions, the close connection between the prayer and divine intervention.

Every priest has experienced mental wandering. The mind when not occupied begins to recall various people (relatives, friends, associates, even enemies). I now realize that frequently God is at work in this wandering.

These wanderings are now scheduled into every day - those times when I let God take my mind wherever He wills - to those people who need intercession. As He recalls them to me, I lift them up to Him and ask His blessings. Frequently these very people call, or come for help.

Jesus thanked the Father, that He had lost no one the Father had given to him, except Judas. Often the priest has worked hard with a person or a family whom he does not see regularly. The priest can wonder if the effort was worthwhile and frequently feels helpless since he no longer has close, personal contact. Yet the heavenly Father doesn't want the priest to lose anyone whom He has given over to him.

So instead of just wondering, or just thinking about parishioners, the priest should come before the Father in intercession for these people.

This power applies especially to retired priests. They should intercede for all those whom they actively helped in past years. The heavenly Father will lead the priest mentally to those for whom he should be praying.

4. "We Threw You In, Too"

Mom has always had her rosary novena and whenever the family needed a special favor, out would come the rosary novena. In 1946, the Bell Telephone was about to go on strike, so out came the rosary novena. A few weeks later, Dad was named to a management position.

Recently, Mom and Dad were deeply immersed again in the rosary novena. Suddenly, my brother Joe got a week off to be home at Christmas and more important, my brother Rich got the perfect job offer with another company.

The day Joe left after Christmas, I was with with them and they then revealed to me how they had entered into this special prayer of intercession. Dad then turned to me and said "Did you feel anything different, because we threw you in, too."

Over the past nine years, I have literally watched the power of intercession before my very eyes. Just recently, we have urged the people to intercede daily in the Church for the parish needs. In this way, a powerful spiritual relationship will exist between priests and people.

A priest with a large weekly healing service also has large intercessory support. Every night, 150 to 200 people intercede for God's power upon the larger crowd that assembles on Sunday evening.

Each Sunday the parish gathers — no need to change or destroy that. The question is — do they gather in power? Does the priest try to minister alone and without intercessory support, or are there people who gather every day in that same Church to seek God's power for the whole parish when they come on Sunday?

17

Power Over Sin

Sin will no longer have power over you; you are now under grace, not under the law. (Rom 6:14)

But thanks be to God who has given us the victory through our Lord, Jesus Christ. (1 Cor. 15:57)

We face in the Church a widespread moral crisis, (so much so that no quoting of statistics is even needed). Because of this problem, Church authorities keep restating the traditional moral standards.

Yet, without the religious experiences freely bestowed by Jesus Christ, to a large measure we are back in Old Testament times — and the Law can still not save.

When Paul wrote to his foolish Galatians, he asked,

> ... *how did you receive the Spirit? Was it through the observance of the law or through faith in what you heard?* (3:2)

Later, he clearly writes —*Have you had such remarkable experiences all to no purpose. . .?* (V4)

As priests we know this theology well. The law cannot free from the power of sin. That freedom lies in Baptism.

> *"All of you have been baptized into Christ have clothed yourselves with Him."* (V27)

But, without religious experiences our Baptism lies dormant — the power of Jesus within us is drained off, dried up.

Without religious experiences, a widespread moral crisis is inevitable when a culture breaks down. The culture can no more be put back together than Humpty-Dumpty. But our faith is not in culture, nor in law but in Jesus who

> *"lavishes the Spirit on you and works wonders in your midst."* (V5)

The following stories picture the widescale and pervasive power of sin, our own powerlessness, and the need for God's power to overcome.

1. "No Such Thing As A Bad Boy"

Last week I visited Father Flanagan's "Boys' Town". His famous saying "There is no such thing as a bad boy" seems naive. But the saying goes further, "There are bad homes, there are bad neighborhoods, there are bad environments."

Sin is like sand that gets into every machine of human life — into every heart, home, school, parish, economic system. Look wherever you wish and you will find its power.

Realizing that sin's power is everywhere, should make the priest seek God's power everywhere. Wherever we look we need that power — in our hearts, our rectories, our schools, our liturgies. We have to teach the people how to yield to God's power.

The world of God's power in religious experiences is given to everyone through Baptism, but it has to be released so God's power can overcome the "bad homes, the bad neighborhoods, the bad environments."

2. Just A Fair Price

Yesterday, a meeting brought together people devoted to the economic problems of the poor nations. Archbishop Helder Camara spoke and his theme was the same word he has been speaking for years — that the international economic system is unjust because it is devised by the rich nations. I had heard the Archbishop speak in Rome in 1965. His words always remained with me, "We don't want your aid, we want a fair price for our goods."

Sin creates unjust systems. Yet what else is expected from a human race in which original sin is universal?

And what do we do in the face of this growing sinful world system? Initiate liturgical reform? Update our Scriptural renewal? Bring out the guitars?

Or do we priests seek God's power? Do we learn how to release God's power in our people? Do we let God equip us?

God has no optional gifts. Religious experiences are not powers we can choose or not choose. They are the needed preparation for overcoming the unjust world systems.

3. *The Evil I Do Not Intend*

Today is January 1, 1981. Today's paper carried the story that the U.S. sold fifteen billion dollars in arms to seventy nations, the highest annual sale in our history, even though President Carter was committed to lowering the amount of U.S. involvement in arming the world.

We calmly read those figures. For many people, who will never read that article, the news really means their death.

The President certainly loved peace. He sought no war and in his heart wanted to reduce the arms level. He is like Paul in the Romans:

"What happens is that I do, not the good I intend
to do, but the evil I do not intend." (6:19)

The question is:

"Who can free me from this body under the power
of death". (V24)

The question is not of good intentions, or good plans, or good theory. The question is the stark and naked one of power.

A moment has to come when the priest realizes that it is a new world and the clock can't be turned back. It is a moment of experienced powerlessness against all that is happening.

God will not leave the priest without power. But if the priest refuses to go deeper; refuses to seek God's face; refuses to accept religious experiences; then he will have only his own powers to fall back upon and will probably end up doing the evil that he did not intend.

4. *"I Used To Fear That Power"*

On a few Saturday nights, I visited a powerful service of a Protestant minister. He had always been a traditional minister in a Protestant denomination. A few years ago, however, he began getting involved with the Holy Spirit. Facing a dilemma of how to minister to everyone, he came up with the idea of a Saturday night worship service that would stress the Holy Spirit and be open to religious experiences.

As a result, every Saturday the buses roll in from far and wide to fill his church with people of all ages and all denominations. Even the young, the high school kids who had formerly turned away from religion, worship and experience God.

One time, after working with him at an ecumenical gathering, he invited me to the motel coffee shop. As we made our way through the motel, we passed the night club area. The rock music blared out at us. He turned to me and said "I used to fear the power of those experiences, until God taught me how to go out and get His power and His experiences."

I knew what he meant, because I had gone through the same thing — great fear that the world's power could draw many people away from God. I no longer have that fear, for God has given to me large crowds, and the power of religious experiences that heal, restore, and bestow a personal knowledge of Jesus Christ.

Those powers of religious experiences are within the Church, but they must be released. The Catholic Church and priesthood have to be committed to fostering religious experiences or else we will sit back in fear and awe of the power of rock music and drugs and mass media that can carry away all our people.

5. An X-Rated Motel

Recently my Tribunal work took me to New Orleans. The motel there provided show-case movies at no extra charge. However, some of these movies were *X-rated.* As we were checking out, I realized the cost of these movies was naturally in the bill. Since then, I have written to the chain, to see what can be done about the built-in evil of helping "X-rated" movie production. In the past I would have let it go. Now, I see clearly the ministry of delivering from evil. I'll try to explain this vision.

Priesthood exists for the salvation of God's people. Many people grow discouraged with gospel ideals because they experience a world loaded with evil — like a plot of ground filled with land mines. Priesthood exists to deliver the people from evil — "to set the captives free."

Too often, we priests look at the gospel demands and then, in our compassion for the people, water down those demands. Instead, we should look at the reasons the demands can't be met. What evil is present? How are we to deliver from evil?

Obviously, none of that will happen unless the priest is experiencing God. Any priest encountering evil, who doesn't walk with God, will be overcome, and end up like the sons of Sceva when they tried an exorcism.

> *"He dealt with them so violently that they fled from his house naked and bruised".* (Acts, 19:16)

6. *Liberty To Captives*

My Newman Club work brought me through the X-rated section of Philadelphia — that part reserved for all the adult movies and book stores.

As I drove through that section, I prayed. Every time, the prayer was harsh and demanding, the prayer of deliverance from evil powers.

Unfortunately, most priests are totally unfamiliar with both the word "deliverance" and the "deliverance prayer." They seldom if ever use any power of deliverance, which is meant to free the people from evil.

Even the best parishioners are enmeshed in multiple and powerful evil. They live in a world that is hopelessly entangled. Jesus understood Himself as fulfilling Isaiah:

> *"The Spirit of the Lord is upon me: therefore he has anointed me. He has sent me.. to proclaim liberty to captives".* (Luke 4:18)

Without religious experiences, we priests will not even realize the pervasive power of evil. We will certainly not be helping our parishioners to find the liberty given by the Spirit.

7. *Breaking The Cycle Of Poverty*

One time, in my first assignment, I came upon a section of about twenty homes in which no one was registered in the parish.

I visited the people to see who might be Catholics. Upon knocking on each door, I was greeted by a cheerful black person. It was difficult to believe, since as in most cities, the blacks in West Chester were usually in the poorer sections of town. Yet here was a beautiful section of homes in suburban West Chester, all owned by black families.

Finally, one man told me the story. These people, too, had lived in that poorer section. Their jobs were the usual ones — gas station attendants, city hall clerks, etc. About eight years previously a group of them saw the economic bondage they were in by just renting poor homes and wasting their money. So they gathered together, sought out a piece of land, borrowed from the bank, parceled up the land and built their own homes. The man concluded the story. "A lot of our own black people laughed at us, saying we were wasting our time, but they are still renting poor homes in a rundown section, and we own our own homes in the suburbs."

These people had seen the unjustness and the evil they were caught in. They also were led to break the bonds of that evil.

Evil is all over the place — built into our homes, our economy, our neighborhoods. Evil is not made by man. It is much more intelligent than man. Sin uses man to build systems of evil in a world made originally by the good God.

The priest, therefore, can't set out like Don Quixote to take on all forms of evil. He has to be led by God. God will bring the priest face to face with certain evils, and the priest will know clearly how he can free his people.

8. *Scarred And Helpless*

Every day I listen to the stories of divorced Catholics seeking an annulment. Over the past five years, one point has stood out — alcoholism, especially the alcoholic problem with the parents of the now divorced young man or woman. Other sources are broken homes, parents lacking affectivity, sometimes just broken parents unable to provide a home.

What we are seeing in Catholic tribunals are scarred people who have suffered evil from others.

Recently a reporter posed as a student at a Philadelphia public high school. Later the paper did a series of articles. Naturally, all kinds of denials came forth from school officials. However a teacher then wrote an even worse report of what was really happening — from marijuana smell in the corridors to violence in the classroom. How many students suffer from that evil?

All are scarred, all are helpless, all share in the problem. Only the power of God can save mankind from all that evil.

A priest who truly sees, has to see the enormous, pervasive power of sin. A priest who truly sees, has to grasp his own helplessness in the face of all that.

That experience should lead him to the feet of Jesus, who will gladly give the priest a power over evil.

18

Power Over Occult

Our battle is not against human forces but against the principalities and powers, the rulers of this world of darkness, the evil spirits in regions above.

(Eph 6:12)

Thus did God disarm the principalities and powers. He made a public show of them and, leading them off captive, triumphed in the person of Christ.

(Col 2:15)

In the Baltimore Catechism and the seminary, some mention was always made of fortune-tellers and occult powers but no great stress was put upon the question, because those phenomena were on the periphera of human life. (Just as drugs were not even mentioned at that time).

The early years of ministry bore this out. I can remember very few times in the first couple of years of priesthood that people had been involved with occult powers.

Now, the seeking after strange powers abounds and although the wave of transcendental meditation and yoga have somewhat subsided — the problem of the occult still permeates society. T.V. programs use it and highlight it — ouija boards, tarot cards, fortune-tellers and a host of other occult powers abound.

The following stories touch briefly on occult involvement, and some who have managed to escape unscathed. This freeing from occult bondage is an area of pastoral care that every priest should know and use when needed.

1. Three Tragedies

I can clearly recall three people who came after seeing fortune-tellers. All of them had serious problems from the event. The story was always the same.

The fortune-teller had told them some true things about their life, and then predicted a future tragedy. Because the "true things" had drawn the people into belief and credence, when the tragedy was predicted, they were like fish who had bitten the hook.

There seemed no way to gain freedom. They had to be told that the tragedies wouldn't happen (occult future-sayers are frequently wrong) and that if they would renounce the experience, the occult power over them would be broken.

All three responded and all three were restored to the peace they had before becoming involved.

2. Astral Projection

A young woman, with a deep Catholic background delved into many things to see if somewhere she could find herself. In a Carribean hotel, she and another stewardess were talking about searching into things. The stewardess asked her if she "ever tried astral-projection."

Since she never had, the stewardess began to lead her through the various steps of this "out of the body" technique. Suddenly she felt some force enter her body. Since the "astral projecting" was taking place in darkness as they were falling asleep, the girl jumped out of bed and turned the lights on. Her friend began to scream because the girl's face was all contorted into an image that approximated what we conceive as the devil. Both of them knelt down and said a Hail Mary.

Fortunately, that brush with evil propelled this young woman to seek God's powers in the charismatic prayer groups. Here, the young woman has found herself. She has a number of extraordinary stories of God's power; and frequently gives talks to large groups.

Like this young stewardess, many people search because the surface answers of the world don't satisfy them. Their searching leads them to involvement with occult powers. Can we priests help these seekers? Do we know the true powers that lead to Jesus' Kingdom?

3. False Tongues

One Saturday evening I attended a Protestant worship service. On Sunday the minister presided over his traditional denominational service. But on Saturdays he filled the Church, as buses came from near and far. In the beautiful worship, God's power could be felt by all.

After the service, he invited people who needed prayers to come forward. People began to stream up. Then, from one side of the church came a disturbance. A girl about eighteen years old was trying to make her way to be prayed over. As she did, a power came over her and she began speaking in false tongues. The sounds were embarassing to her and totally disruptive of the worship. Finally, some people took her aside quietly and prayed over her. She became calm and freed of the evil.

What happened was really easily recognized by anyone familiar with deliverance. The story was much like the gospel – where evil, in the presence of God's power, is forced to manifest itself. In coming to the surface, evil then becomes vulnerable. The power of the worship and the girl's seeking prayers, brought the evil to the surface where it could be dealt with.

Evil is ingrained and hidden, powerful yet unnoticed. This evil comes to light when God's power is present.

Evil never worries when the power of God is absent. It easily coexists with the human and even disguises itself as humanly good.

Our liturgies should manifest God's power. If that happens, then the evil ingrained in the people will become evident and able to be dealt with. The manifestation need not be spectacular.

Everyone at a Sunday liturgy needs to be delivered from hidden evils, large or small. A liturgy without God's power, doesn't even evoke the first stage of that deliverance – forcing the evil to come to the surface, and at least helping the people to see how they are not free.

4. "He Gave Me A New Gift"

A young man got involved with the prayer group and his influence was not always a good one. Later we began a young adult group in another area and he also showed up there. Soon the group was feeling the effects of his presence, so I had to ask him to leave that young group and return to his original group.

A few weeks later, he was waiting for me before the prayer meeting, saying that he "had been given a new gift". He took out his book. I saw page after page with what looked like Hebrew. Some space on each page was not written on. Gradually the unwritten parts got longer and the forms of various images got clearer and clearer – most of the forms were pigs' heads.

The young man explained that whenever he put his pen to the paper it moved along and this language was written and the images formed. Fortunately, I understood the gift well, but the power was from evil sources. The gift was counterfeit.

The Church has always been clear about "supernatural powers." Sometimes these powers come from God. However, other powers come from sources besides God. Today, many Catholics dabble greatly in strange, supernatural phenomenon. Ouija boards, tarot cards, Edgar Cayce books, doctrines on reincarnation, mind control, transcendental meditation, and a host of other avenues into strange powers with no connection to Jesus Christ abound. These are affecting many Catholics.

5. Strange Phenomenon

Sometimes, these strange powers are present in children whose homes are used for seances. Among Italian people there is the "evil eye" and among the Spanish people there is the "bruja".

This "seeking of powers" militates against the Lordship of Jesus, and turns the person away from Jesus.

There are thousands who see these "strange powers" as "neutral ground", of no harm to their religious practices. Some people make the daily horoscope their bible reading, and are really in bondage to what they read each day.

The priest has to be aware of these problems. He has to preach clearly against them, and be able to help his people who have been involved.

6. *Open To Everything?*

After a parish adult education lecture, a person asked about astrology. In trying to adopt an attitude of "openness to everything" I replied that I didn't know much about the topic, but there seemed to be "something there."

A deeper immersion into religious experiences, however, demanded a far sharper discernment than just "being open to everything," including astrology.

Religious experiences should bring a discernment of good and evil. A heightened awareness of God brings a sharper focus on His world. The only way to deal with the world is to see it clearly for what it is — a mixture of good and evil, of grace and sin, of mankind reaching for the highest ideals or stooping to the lowest depths.

The God I experience is a freeing God. Evil and sin are bondage. In the light of religious experiences I can't remain neutral about evil that spreads confusion and darkness.

This perception of good and evil is basic to ministry. Any priest who feels that his parish is doing fine because a high percentage attends mass, not only lacks discernment of good and evil — he doesn't even know what is going on.

A valid ministry results only from an immersion into the people's lives. "Immersion" doesn't just mean we are there with them. "Immersion" means we bring discernment of good and evil.

I truly believe that many priests' ministry is connected with discovering the one good that God is calling the priest to bring forth or the one evil that God is calling him to deal with. That one good or evil is the door to his whole priesthood.

Part Six

Religious
Experiences
and Charisms

On Easter Friday, 1971, I called Brother Pancratius Boudreau C.SS.R. known affectionately as Panky, to find out the time of his weekly prayer meeting. Almost two weeks had passed since Palm Sunday when, through the words of my sister-in-law, I knew I had to join what was then called Catholic Pentecostalism.

From that moment, when all the lights went on, I also knew that I should go to Panky's group since it was the movement's center and would provide a good teaching on this new phenomenom.

His first words to me were "Weren't you here about a year ago?" "About six months ago ' I replied. After hanging up, I realized I had been there one year to the day — Easter Friday, 1970.

The two weeks of being drawn to Panky's group gave way to wonderment that I was returning on the anniversary of my first casual acquaintance with the prayer group.

That night, as I parked the car my thoughts went back exactly one year. At that time, I had experienced just a small group attending mass. That night I never thought of coming back. Yet, here I was, not only back but knowing that "this was it".

So, I stood outside the doors of St. Boniface saying to myself "What a difference one year makes. Last year, this meant nothing. Now I know that everything I am; everything I will be; my whole past, my whole present, my whole future, my whole priesthood, and my whole eternity is tied up with what is behind those doors, and I don't even know what goes on behind those doors."

What was "behind those doors" was a ministry in the Spirit. It has been ten years now, and I don't know what would have happened to me if I had never gone through those doors and experienced charisms.

The following three chapters on charisms are very limited, since I have already written extensively on the subject (cf. A Key to Charismatic Renewal in the Catholic Church). Yet, a book on experiencing God has to include charisms because those gifts are "God experiences" flowing over into service to others.

19

Knowing The Charisms

---

*Now, brothers, I do not want to leave you in
ignorance about the spiritual gifts.*

(1 Cor 12:1)

My 1971 involvement in the prayer group, caused me to scurry for the theology books and scriptural commentaries. The teachings were always there — Tanqueray in "The Spiritual Life" explained clearly the classical list of charisms in 1 Cor C12. The Scriptural commentaries had their usual exegesis on the meaning of each gift, and the Catholic Encyclopedia had all its articles on charisms. Charisms were part and parcel of Catholic tradition.

Yet where were the charisms in the Catholic Church? Who even knew of them? I remembered a fleeting reference to speaking in tongues given during a theology class.

I thought healings were limited to saints and their canonization process (and I knew how hard they were to prove). From time to time I heard of a miraculous event, but the story was generally hard to pin down.

Before 1971, I certainly didn't expect the charismatic intervention of the Spirit, and I didn't know of any other priest who did either.

Now, the charisms are a regular part of my ministry. The following stories are written so every priest would at least want to know more about charisms.

1. Can You Still Commit Sin?

The dumbest question I ever heard about praying in tongues came from a priest. Four of us were having a late night discussion during our annual retreat. One priest had read about Catholic Pentecostalism and was asking intelligent questions. Two others had no background at all so they remained passive spectators.

At the end, the priest asked to be prayed over for the Baptism of the Spirit and the gift of prayer tongues. I asked the other two to join the prayer. Toward the end, I prayed in tongues helping the priest to yield to the gift. At this point came the dumbest question. The one priest, somewhat amazed at the whole phenomena, looked at me and asked "After you can do that, can you still commit sin"? I assured him that we could. Since then, that priest also has yielded to the gift.

The point brings out the widespread ignorance among priests, even about the basic gift of Pentecost. Regarding charisms, as with any powers, there are some highly sophisticated teachings and experiences that no one would expect every priest to know. But praying in tongues is the basic gift – a first fruit of religious experiences. The ignorance of this gift is widespread.

The following statement might sound radical, but it has to be said:

"Praying in tongues seems to be available for everyone. It is a primary result of religious experiences. Without prayer tongues, it is difficult for religious experiences to grow or mature and it seems impossible for charisms to be present in any degree of power or frequency. The lack of prayer tongues in the Catholic Church is eloquent testimony to the lack of religious experiences and charisms."

That statement is not harsh. It's a true picture about the present state of religious experiences, charisms and prayer tongues in the Catholic Church. The dumbest question I ever heard sums up the primary problem – a lack of knowledge among priests.

"After you can do that, can you still commit sin?"

2. *The Port Richmond People*

Last night, I met with six leaders of a new prayer group in the Port Richmond section of Philadelphia. Port Richmond is a blue-collar section where sophistication doesn't flourish, but gives way to a down-to-earth approach to life. During the evening one of the women even commented "Father, don't forget you're dealing with people from Port Richmond."

They were from Port Richmond, but they knew how to use God's powers. Twenty people have been coming together for a year and a half, and this meeting was to see if the group was ready to become open to the parish.

Their questions were clear and showed they understood the various charisms. They delineated the gift of tongues, interpretation, prophetic tongues and prophecy, and discernment of tongues.

They confirmed my deepest beliefs — that very simple people could enjoy religious experiences and learn to use charisms. As I answered their basic questions, it dawned on me that at least 95% of the priests in the United States wouldn't even know what they were talking about.

My dream is that all that changes; that priests will know as much about religious experiences as they do about liturgy; and as much about the charisms as they do about sacramental theology.

3. *Is The Gospel For Real?*

In the 1960's and 1970's many called the New Testament miracles into question. Some scholars said that the multiplication of the loaves and fishes was really a story of the power of charity, namely, Jesus shared his food and everyone else who brought food with them also shared what they had.

Sudden healings through exorcism were seen as Jesus having an overwhelming personality who effected a total personal reintegration by his psychological powers.

Everything was questioned — the lame walking, the blind seeing, the reality of the visions.

Since the Church in the 1960's had none of these manifestations, a certain distance existed between personal experiences and the New Testament.

For the last 10 years, my world and the New Testament world have not been that distant. I have either directly experienced or met other people who have directly experienced every miracle in the New Testament except the raising from the dead — and that includes the direct multiplication of food and the healing of the blind.

To debunk New Testament miracles is ridiculous since the same things are happening in our day, in Jesus' name.

Religious experiences are the door to the New Testament world. However, these gospel powers are available only by the priest's personal awakening. So priests should seek first to experience the Kingdom, and to know that New Testament power is available for their ministry.

4. The Importance Of 1 Cor. C14

Each week at the priest prayer group, we follow Paul's teaching, "You can all speak your prophecies, but one by one, so that all may be instructed and encouraged." (1 Cor 14:31)

The priests gather, believing in faith that during the hours of praise God will speak to them. In fact, the priest's prayer meeting without prophecy would long ago have disbanded, verifying Paul's injunction "Set your hearts on spiritual gifts — above all, the gift of prophecy." (VI)

So there we are, gathered around, hands upraised, praising God in a tongue we don't understand, and waiting for God to speak to us. Sounds foolish, and without 1 Cor C14, the practice would probably be hard to justify, even scripturally.

These priests are a living witness to the importance of 1 Cor C14. However, that chapter is in everyone's bible and it doesn't seem that it should be limited to an evening prayer group. A central question, which only priests can answer is, "When will the power of 1 Cor C14 be available at the parish liturgy." Paul writes "when you assemble", (and the liturgy is when the Catholic Church assembles), one has a psalm, another some instruction to give, still another a revelation to share; one speaks in a tongue, another interprets" (V26).

5. *Contemplata Aliis Tradere (Giving To Others After Contemplation)*

The Catholic Church has always upheld the value and importance of contemplation. The only more excellent life is when the contemplation overflows into action. "Contemplata aliis tradere".

Religious experiences fully unfold into service, usually following a pattern.

1) A stage of withdrawal into the joy of the experiences themselves.
2) Self-enlightenment and personal change.
3) Growth in the experiences.
4) A desire for ministry and service to the Church.
5) The receiving of charisms.

This is not a charismatic renewal book, but charisms are deeply connected to religious experiences. They are God's power in ministry. For a priest not to want charisms, is not to want God's power.

Religious experiences, the priest's identity and the priest's charisms are just 3 phases of the same divine inner working.

20

Seeking The Gifts

Set your hearts on spiritual gifts — above all, the gift of prophecy.

(1 Cor C 14:1)

Say not, "I am too young". To whomever I send you, you shall go; whatever I command you, you shall speak.

(Jer 1 7)

Then I heard the voice of the Lord saying, "Whom shall I send? Who will go for us?" "Here I am," I said, "send me!"

(Is. 6:8)

The teaching for newcomers at a prayer meeting always discusses prayer tongues. Most people are surprised, as I was, that the gift is for everyone. As this teaching begins to dawn on them, that becoming part of a prayer group involves praying in tongues, the inevitable question is asked, "Why do I need that?"

The priest could ask the same question about charisms in his ministry, "Why do I need those?"

The answer, especially in these days, is not hard to come by, We priests, consciously or unconsciously, live now by lowered expectations. We just don't expect to happen what used to happen. We don't expect people to listen to our moral teachings, or to come to our confessional, or to join the societies that used to flourish, or to fill the Church for the annual mission (which in most places doesn't even exist any more).

So, we priests do what nature teaches us to do to survive — we adjust. We lower our sights. We don't even expect many vocations because the full role of priesthood is limited now. Our wings have been cut, and we are satisfied with just walking instead of flying.

That is why we need charisms. The crowds return when they know God is once more acting among His people.

The following stories urge the priest to seek these gifts — not for his own glory but because the people need God s powers.

1. "I Want All The Gifts"

During my fifth week at a prayer meeting, a group was praying over a few people. As they prayed, I just knew I had to seek charismatic gifts. The feeling was so strong that I sat down in the chair, looked up at them and said, "I want all the gifts."

That statement wasn't selfish. It was the desperate appeal of a priest who had seen the power of the gifts and knew what they could do for his people.

It strikes me as strange that priests have difficulties with regard to prophecy or healing or miracles. It should be just the opposite. They should want these powers with all their hearts for the good of their people.

Is there no sick person in the priest's parish? No weak person in the parish? No one hardened in sin? No one without problems?

No one learns to swim standing at poolside, and God isn't going to give charisms to priests who don't seek them.

2. In The Twinkling Of An Eye

At a Regional Canon Law convention, a special seminar on Charismatic Renewal was given. One priest shared his story,

He was about to leave the active ministry, but felt he should go to confession before taking the final step. Fortunately he ended up talking to a priest who believed in charisms. Instead of trying to talk him out of the decision, the confessor just asked him to spend a few minutes with him in prayer. With that, everything changed. The darkness lifted and the confusion was gone. He was suddenly happier than he had been for years and at peace in remaining in his vocation. Over the years, I have met the priest often, so the gift was not just a passing, emotional high.

Some powerful, lasting gifts can be bestowed in just a moment or a few minutes. This violates most of our thinking that lasting changes can come only slowly. Many times, God's gifts are given "in a moment", "in the twinkling of an eye."

It would be totally unfair to preach to the people that every problem will receive an instant answer. But its equally unfair to believe that God's help is far off, or way down the road, or able to bring change only slowly. As the priest experiences this world of

God's power, nothing will surprise him — even instant changes that last a lifetime.

3. Praying Right Away

One night a man came to me after our prayer meeting. We had a mutual friend named Mary. In a simple request he said, "Mary is sick. Could you pray with me?" A group of us prayed for her. It was 11:15 P.M.

The next day I called to find out what hospital Mary was in, because the description the night before was of serious stomach difficulties. Mary herself answered the phone. At 11:15 the night before all the pain suddenly left and she had fallen asleep for 12 hours. Later, she went to a doctor and x-rays showed she had a healed ulcer.

The act of prayer that night was a simple one. No great effort was used. No one strained hard to "have enough faith". No one "claimed a healing was going to occur". We just prayed together in faith.

Every priest can do that. He just has to believe in the power of actually praying. People frequently come up to the priest, relate a personal difficulty or concern, with the final request to "please say a prayer". Usually, the priest promises to do that. What we should do is just stop, there and then, and pray with the person for that need. The results will be surprising.

4. "The Dabitur"

In preparing the sermon for Holy Family Sunday, I tried to outline the picture of a good home. However, during the homily I was led to talk about something not in the prepared text — the importance of choosing the right partner. While doing this, I was even wondering to myself why this was happening. I found out after mass.

A young woman came up for help. She was to marry in three weeks and was filled with fears. She didn't know if these were the usual pre-marital jitters, or if something was wrong with the relationship. An interview disclosed serious problems, especially with her fiancee. We both agreed she should call off the marriage.

When Paul wrote "To one the Spirit gives wisdom in discourse, to another the power to express knowledge" (1 Cor C12 – V8), he was asking us priests to let the Spirit give us words.

For myself, this gift of anointed words is usually given on Saturday evening when the sermon is being written. So strongly does a given point come – forgiveness, alcoholism, abortion, care for children – that deep in my heart I know someone in the congregation needs to hear that word.

The gift is for the people and Jesus is their primary shepherd. Jesus cares for the people through charisms.

To be closed to charisms; not to be open to them; to live in ignorance of these Spirit powers, limits Jesus' powers for His people.

5. The Real Question About Prophecy

On a couple of occasions, priests have questioned prophecy. One priest said he believed in "divine enlightenment" but not prophecy. By that, he meant that God certainly enlightens, but He would not give words for someone to speak.

Another priest used to have innumerable problems with the use of the gift.

On one occasion, at a meeting of 50 theologians concerning Charismatic Renewal, a bishop came over after a prayer service and asked who gave me permission to prophesy.

The three stories show three different attitudes toward prophecy – to deny it can take place, to legitimately question it, and to call into question the very right to use the gift.

But the biggest question goes unanswered – if prophecy is the gift that most builds up the Church, why do so many bishops and priests know so little about it?

6. "Being Born Again" Not Enough

I met "Holy Hubert" at a full Gospel luncheon. At first, he looked like a bum, complete with some front teeth missing. However, it only took a few seconds to see that he was anything but that. The missing teeth were due to beatings on the campus of

Berkeley as he witnessed to Jesus Christ against Jerry Rubin and the "free speech" movement.

We spent an hour together and he hold me his story. He had been an extremely successful gospel preacher in the South, somewhat comparable to Billy Graham, complete with a team and gigantic crusades.

He had been "born again" but had stayed away from the charismatic aspects of religious experiences until one night in the quiet basement of his Church he allowed himself to pray in tongues. Then God began to speak to him and led him to Berkeley. He called his people together to tell them that the Crusades were over, that everything was disbanded and that he was to go to Berkeley.

The first year on campus, a free speech rally was held every day. Regularly, Holy Hubert would take the microphone to preach Jesus Christ. Well, "free speech" seemed to be a limited concept to Jerry Rubin, because Hubert always got beat up for his use of it. Once or twice during that first year he almost was killed. The year ended with about 15 trips to the hospital and no converts.

Then things turned around. Some who had almost killed him, became his converts and even saved his life.

I haven't met Holy Hubert since, but his story has a lot to say. If he had just stopped at a religious experience level, the whole work at Berkeley would never have come about. He would still be preaching Southern crusades.

7. *Fulfilling Religious Experiences*

Personal religious experiences, and even leading others into those experiences, are not the final step. A breakthrough happens in ministry when the priest opens himself up to charisms. The gifts are the normal manifestations of the Spirit, the clearest and most powerful way for Jesus to teach, to empower and to guide.

Even many of the "born-again" churches won't touch the charisms, since they are too hot for them to handle. But the Catholic Church accepts them easily and, when integrated wth sacraments, theology and traditional teaching, they create no grave problems.

8. *Praying With People*

Eight hundred people gathered at a special day of renewal. After Communion, I took the microphone to go down among them to pray. On this occasion, the prayer centered on the return of children to the sacraments. By the end of the prayer, people were crying all over the Church. Afterward, I asked about the extraordinary result of that simple prayer. A woman replied "Father, I guess you don't know it, but in this area the biggest heartache of many parents is that their children don't go to mass anymore. There is nothing more sought by these people than their children's return to the sacraments."

For the past nine years, when the situation allows, I have prayed for the congregation after Holy Communion. But it's not just any prayer. Enlightenment comes and definite gifts are sought from God.

The priest should frequently pray for and with his people. The settings are both liturgical and informal. It is a shame if the priest doesn't know how to be led by God to pray for what the people need.

21

Experiencing Charisms

"I solemnly assure you, the man who has faith in me will do the works I do, and greater far than these".   (Jn. 14:12)

The spirit of the Lord shall rest upon him:
> *a spirit of wisdom and of understanding,*
> *a spirit of counsel and of strength,*
> *a spirit of knowledge and of fear of the Lord.*   (Is 11:12)

Introduction

In the seminary, I never dreamed that anyone would be healed by any prayer that I would say. That was a saint's domain.

I heard the stories of John Vianney reading hearts, but that was something special.

Priesthood for me was going to be visiting the people; being available to guide, forgive and console; and giving a Sunday sermon. All of those still happen, yet everything is changed. The power in my ministry is God's, through gifts called charisms.

Not every priest has every charism, but every priest has some gift — not just on the human level, and not just on the Church level, but on the Spirit level of a direct action of God upon the priest to serve the people.

The following stories describe charisms and encourage priests to begin using them.

1. Who Doesn't Need To Be Healed?

About fifty girls and a few religious were attending mass at a boarding school. The gospel was about Jesus healing. Because the group was small I felt free to ask just how many needed to be healed. Just 2 raised their hands — one had a sore wrist and the other an upset stomach.

The truth really was that all of them needed to be healed, since everyone is hurt on some level.

The healing power of Jesus is limited when:

1)   So few realize they need to be healed.
2)   So few believe that Jesus will heal.
3)   So many are reluctant to seek God's healing.

And because healing is such an "emotional issue", we priests don't want to get near it.

The most difficult emotional problem for a priest is to be presented with an obvious physical difficulty and be asked to pray for healing.

At that point, the priest conjures up the T.V. healer scene, and begins to wonder how it is done. These emotional difficulties with healing are understandable, yet healing seems best handled by priests.

Personally, I don't claim any special ministry of healing, but people have been healed on every level. The biggest news, however, is that this healing is nothing special but is a regular part of the priesthood.

2. Healing Through Tears

I used to pride myself that I never cried. Even during the funeral of John Kennedy, when everyone else was going around red-eyed. I held back the tears. The Lord has changed all that.

This healing through tears began when I was at the end of a winter cold. Unknowingly the confinement and inactivity had begun to burden me. On Sunday afternoon, as I was getting ready to return to work, I came together with others to pray. One person had a word from the Lord that I was to cry. Strangely enough, since that was how I felt, I let the tears come. For more than twenty minutes they came. I returned home, fell soundly asleep and reported to work the next day feeling totally refreshed.

The next healing through tears was much longer, and happened on a weekend retreat. The tears began on Friday night as the Lord showed me the burdens I was carrying. The process continued on Saturday morning and again on Sunday morning, as the healing through tears was completed. Through the gift, the memories that unknowingly got lodged in my system — even in the muscles and tissues — were washed out, and in their place was a total wholeness.

Sometime later, I was watching a discussion by professional masseuses. One was saying how muscles hold memories, in the sense that during tense situations we manipulate the body so that certain body muscles are associated with certain burdens. As these professional masseuses would relieve the muscles, the person would cry — not from pain but from emotional release. Their process went from muscle release to tears. Our gift went from tears to muscle release.

From time to time now, as I kneel before the Eucharist, the Lord will explain that I have to cry. He will bring events before my eyes that have unknowingly been burdensome and then He washes them out by His tears. The gift is usually over in a few minutes and then God's word can come in a new freshness.

3. Everyone Can Ask Jesus

One day, a woman asked me to heal her eleven year old daughter who every night had nightmares. Healing was still new to me. The girl's father had died two years before, and besides this he had an alcohol problem. The girl loved both her parents deeply.

A year earlier I would have used Frankel's Logotherapy or Rodgers' counseling techniques. However, after our short discussion, she and I just talked to Jesus about them. A couple weeks later, the mother called and said the girl was healed. I have met both of them over the next few years and the nightmares have not returned.

A few days later, I was called to another little girl who, for some reason, had refused to eat for the previous three days. The family had been consulting a psychiatrist, but because this was now Sunday evening, they were left on their own. Heartened by the other success with a little girl, I did the same thing – talked a little while and then had the little girl pray to Jesus. Whatever the problem, she immediately was freed to resume eating.

Both cases involved just half an hour and to this day I still don't know what caused the girl not to eat. At that time I knew very little about healing, and even now, still know very little. There was nothing sensational about the prayers. No special formula was used. Just two people asking Jesus to help.

I write these stories because any priest can do that much, and every priest should do that much whenever someone comes with a problem. This doesn't preclude other helps that might be at hand – good advice or someone who would have a natural answer or solution. But the priest should also ask Jesus for help, and have the person ask also. The healing power of Jesus is not meant to be obscure or wrapped in great mystery.

4. "I Will Give You The Gift"

Within weeks after I had joined the Charismatic Movement and prayed in tongues, the prophetic gift began to emerge. One night I asked God openly for this gift. Within seconds, the words came clearly. "Stay away from the world, and I will give you the gift". Even without the promise aspect, the saying makes sense. If the mind is filled with worldy news and entertainment, little room remains for God's word.

I would like to describe the prophetic gift, because I believe the power is there for many priests. The process is a very simple one – much like a child seeking words from a parent.

First, there must be inner stillness. Attachments or hurt feelings or ambitions destroy the gift. This inner stillness is a resting in God's presence and being open to His will.

Secondly, the gift is closely connected with prayer tongues which quickly settle the person and move the mind into the Spirit.

When stilled and settled, and with heart and mind moving quickly into the Spirit, the gift can begin, possibly in just a few seconds.

Sometimes the gift is personal, that is, for myself, and God explains what He is doing and why. This comes sometimes in pictures, with different scenes, usually associated with my favorite field or stream. In the deep portion of the gift, everything works at once — pictures, words, imagination and intellect.

I then have to rely on my feelings, past religious experiences and discernment, to decide if this inner activity:

1) is just my imagination running wild;
2) is my imagination reaching out to God;
3) is God bestowing his prophetic gift.

The same process occurs when praying with people — only now the gift is serving another, as God explains a present need or a gift He is bestowing.

There is never perfect certitude concerning prophecy, and great discernment is needed to distinguish what is known by natural knowledge and what is truly from God. Often the person has to be helped to know what God really means by the words.

Some safeguards for the gift:

Prophecy is not a toy to be played with, and it is not a religious E.S.P.

Prophecy is connected to religious experience and the gift of prayer tongues.

Prophecy is yielded to gradually until the full gift unfolds.

Prophecy is a communal gift, most safely bestowed and used in a group where many people use the gift.

Prophecy is not sought for itself, but as a service to others.

Prophecy is only completely safeguarded when submitted regularly to authority.

Prophecy has been important to us. Without this gift, many works would have never started and those started would never have been completed. So much has only been accomplished through the powerful gift of prophecy.

5. *Give Me The Words*

My brother, Joe, has spent most of his professional life in various parts of the country. As a result, we have established a strong telephone relationship. In the beginning this was just a talking about the questions. Then I began to pray with him and eventually prayed in tongues. Later, I used the gift of prophecy, but put the words in the form of prayer. Later I would use the prophetic form. Last night Joe called and after we talked, he said "Do you think you can get those words for me?"

I had never explained "prophecy" to Joe, nor even used the word. By "get those words", Joe meant prophecy and was saying in his own way that "those words" had meant a lot to him.

This telephone relationship shows the various steps of God's power — first, human advice; then prayer; and finally the complete openness to God's power in the charisms.

6. "It Just Goes Away"

One time, I was asked to pray over a very disturbed woman. The woman was not at all psychotic, but just terribly at odds with herself, having just recently come to the prayer meeting.

I asked the woman what her problems were. As she would mention them, I would say a simple prayer asking God to remove that problem. When we were finished, she looked up and said "I don't understand. You just say "go away" and it goes." Since then, the woman has had great peace. By that event, I was introduced to the prayer of deliverance.

This charism confronts two realities — Satan and bondage. I am not sure they are the same, or coextensive, but certain stories of deliverance are very similar to the gospel experiences of Jesus when He confronted evil spirits. Other stories are much lighter in nature. In both cases freedom results from the deliverance prayer.

7. *A Day Of Anxiety*

I awoke one day anxious about a certain physical condition that I knew was not serious. However, I could not convince myself of that. All day long the anxiety stayed with me, reaching its peak that evening as I was getting ready for the seminary prayer meeting.

Getting into the car, I began to pray in tongues, which became deliverance prayers. The tongues got louder and more harsh. While driving I found myself shouting at the top of my voice. Suddenly the prayer was over, the anxiety left and peace overwhelmed me.

Many things I do not know about deliverance prayer or bondage. I do know the Kingdom of Darkness is real and the gift of religious experiences would be destroyed if I didn't grasp that "Our battle is not against human forces, but against the principalities and powers, the rulers of this world of darkness, the evil spirits in regions above". (Eph 6:12)

8. How Is Your Mother Taking The Change?

One time I was talking to a woman who, by force of circumstances had to leave one religious community for another. She had begun to manifest signs of depression and other difficulties. I knew the problem was her refusal to face the hurt of the whole situation. According to her "everything was fine". Having come to the end of my rope, I turned to God and asked what to do. The words came "Ask her how her mother took the change".

As I asked her "How is your mother accepting all this?" the sister broke into deep sobs that lasted a good fifteen minutes. She was finally ready to face the biggest difficulty of the whole process – that her mother just was not accepting her decision.

Our priestly ministry depends on charisms. Without them, some people will just not be helped.

9. Do We Loaf?

The difficulty with charisms is that they require a high level of human cooperation. The more "human cooperation" is needed, the quicker that action of the Spirit seems to be pushed into the background.

Charisms are intense actions of the Spirit which demand a total human yielding — probably that is why they are always fading in and out of Church life. The Spirit always is at work, it is we who loaf on the job.

There are three levels of human cooperation:

1) Learning about the charisms — by reading, hearing talks, and experiencing the gifts in others.

2) Seeking the charisms — by seeing that they are important for ministry, and by wanting to have these gifts.

3) Yielding to the charisms — by actually beginning to experience these powers.

The difficulty for every priest is the constant temptation to put away the charisms, to lose the vision of what can be in the face of the reality that is.

Charisms complete religious experiences. Without them the other parts of the gift seem to unravel, come apart, and even the religious gifts that were given, seem to get lost.

Charisms are not optional. Without them, the priest can lose everything ". . from those who have not, what little they have will be taken away." (Mk 4:25)

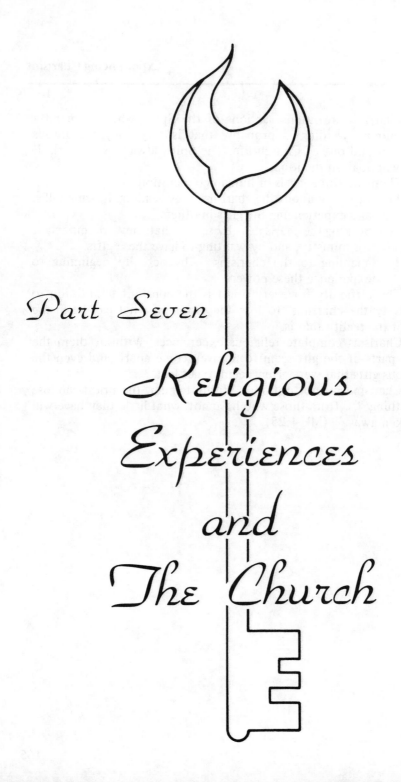

Part Seven

Religious

Experiences

and

The Church

This section is short, not because I have written extensively, but because I have little to write. Ultimately, long-range results will not come from priests experiencing God, or even experiencing charisms.

The full Davidic anointing will happen when religious experiences and charisms are so much a part of the Church's life that everyone will know the Lord, and everyone will experience the Spirit.

It seems that the ideal of universal religious experiences and widespread charisms was possible when the Church was young. On Pentecost, at least, the first hundred and twenty members shared a religious experience, and those experiences remained a clear goal of pastoral care — "Did you receive the Holy Spirit when you became believers?" (Acts 19:2). With the quick expansion of the Church, possibly the loss of religious experiences was inevitable.

In the era of mass communication, the Church again has an opportunity to seek the ideal of universal religious experiences.

However, in a hierarchically structured Church, this will only happen when the priesthood sees that ideal as possible and important. Priests minister to people but they also are the bearers of Church teaching. Religious experiences will only enter the Church itself through its priesthood.

The following chapters describe the beginning of a dream — when not just priests, but the Church herself reaches again for that ideal of universal religious experiences.

22

Church Power
In Baptism

Paul then explained, "John's baptism was a baptism of repentance.   He used to tell the people about the one who would come after him in whom they were to believe -- that is, Jesus.   When they heard this, they were baptized in the name of the Lord Jesus."   (Acts 19:4-5)

I have baptized you in water; he will baptize you in the Holy Spirit.   (MK 1:8)

. . .Jesus was at prayer after likewise being baptized, the skies opened and the Holy Spirit descended on him in visible form like a dove
                                    (LK 3:21-22)

Everywhere the Church seeks power — not for selfish aims but because She is the New Israel and God's instrument of salvation to all the nations.

"Everywhere" means in programs, enlightened theology, updated liturgies, social involvement, speaking on important issues, new codes of laws, new gatherings of bishops, papal travels. All are legitimate forms of seeking to renew and influence.

In looking "everywhere," the Church overlooks the power God places in the people when they are baptized. The importance of releasing Baptismal power is minimized.

Paul teaches clearly that uniting people in the Church comes from Baptism, "It is in one Spirit that all of us, whether Jew or Greek, slave or free, were baptized into one body." (1 Cor 12:13)

The following stories try to describe that overlooked source of power and to urge priests to understand the gifts that are given at the very beginning through Christian initiation.

1. Nobody Is Leaving

On a September weekend in 1980, we were holding our first large Charismatic Conference at the Philadelphia Civic Center. A tremendous priest, who regularly took care of large Archdiocesan Conventions (I think this was his 82nd time at the Civic Center) was handling all the behind-the-scenes preparations.

On Saturday evening, I asked him how things were going. He said, "This is amazing. I have never seen anything like it. Nobody is leaving."

Later in that evening, he came up and asked "I have to prepare the hosts for tomorrow's liturgy. How many of these people will be back?" (The Conference was a commuter event and the people had already come Friday night and Saturday). In confidence I replied "They'll all be back". Sure enough, the next morning the cars and buses rolled into the Civic Center and 7500 people were there on Sunday, too.

What made them come back? Why did they stay? What held them together? They stayed and they came back because they were experiencing God.

As the three days went by, the main hall became like a magnet. No one wanted to miss what was happening. The people chose to sit close to one another, as if the physical closeness was part of what God was doing; or as if being physically separated from Body, the person would miss the power.

That Body was put together over a ten year period. The people who used gifts of service had prayed in a hidden way for years. The people themselves came prepared from their own small weekly gatherings in the Spirit.

Each person brought the released power of his Baptism. Forming christian community is God's gift, part of sacramental Baptism. If Baptism's primary personal gift of a religious experience is never released, the christian community will never exist in the parish. Christian community is rooted in Baptism and begins to come forth by the Baptismal experience. No other foundation exists. No other need be sought. Don't bother looking anywhere else except Baptism.

We don't yet understand all the power in the words, "I baptize you in the name of the Father, and of the Son and of the Holy Spirit."

2. *The Universal Experience*

In 1964, at a three day meeting of chaplains (priests and ministers) to medical schools, I experienced a variety of tongues. The tongues were not those associated with Charismatic Renewal. They were ideas spoken from such diverse experiences and theologies that nobody in the room could talk with anybody else.

By the second day, as things were going so poorly, I asked myself what was wrong. It then dawned on me that I was experiencing Babel, since no central core experience united any of us.

Today, in the United States, that same fragmentation abounds. Right now, because of the explosion of television, we stand at the beginning of unparalled fragmentation. This technology is not evil, but it does present the human race with unforseen futuristic problems, symbolized biblically by Babel.

Every grouping needs a core experience, or else individuals selfishly go their own way. Before technology, the family, neighborhood and parish provided these core experiences. With technology, a person can have his daily experiences away from other people. The family, neighborhood and parish have lost their binding force. We can no longer call people to oneness by their cultural experience, because everyone's cultural experience is now technologically multiplied and diverse. Yet at the core of our Church, at the heart of priestly ministry, is the central experience of Jesus Christ.

Every baptized person possesses the seed of the basic Christian experience. The other core experiences are breaking down, and any attempt to build upon them will wash away. Yet the priest is not left empty. Jesus himself will be the religious experience.

"It pleased God to make absolute fullness reside in him, and by means of him, to reconcile everything in his person...."

(Col 1:19-20)

3. *In South Philadelphia*

A priest attempting to update his theology after Vatican II attended a course on Christian community. Finally, he asked the professor "Would you please define Christian community?"

After receiving a carefully worded theological response, the priest remarked, "That's what we always had in South Philadelphia."

The priest was right. We had Christian community — the close-knit Philadelphia neighbrohood that centered everything on parish and Catholic school. But that was in the 40's and 50's.

Now the modular-family, the often-moved executive, and rootless suburbia are the common experiences. Add to those, the climbing divorce rate where even the basic family unit is destroyed, and Christian community is something "we used to have."

In biology, a great step happens when cells unite and multicellular species begin. Even the human body exists because cells can come together and then specialize into functions. The beginning of "coming together" in Christ's Body lies in Baptism and the beginning religious experience.

4. *Baptism Into Community*

Recently some priests were discussing a television interview of a Latin American bishop. The bishop stressed that Church renewal depended upon small Christian communities that could develop their credal beliefs flowing from a common experience. Others would say that small Christian communities aren't the only approach. However, all say that the baptized should be part of some Christian community.

Religious experiences are closely linked with Christian community. A priest has to accept the beginning religious experience. He also has to accept others into his life who share the same experience.

All community is based on a common experience. The most basic experience is local, the daily experience of living in the same neighborhood.

The common Christian experience begins at Baptism. If this experience is superficial, then the Church will be a surface grouping, able to be brought together from time to time, but for the most part scattered and existing only in theory.

Christian community is not built solely upon the beginning religious experience. However, attempts to try to build a Christian community without a Baptismal experience are futile.

5. Gathering The Parish

A few years ago, at our diocesan workshop, a priest explained the survey results connected to the National Catechical Directory. Especially important was the question of adult religious education, that most difficult of parish tasks.

The survey showed that successful adult religious education occurred only when the teaching was accompanied by a prayer experience.

These results show how helpless we are to call our people together. We possess no power to form Christian community, even with the most intelligent adult programs. The long-term coming together requires a prayer experience.

If priests don't understand the religious experience contained in Baptism, even those people who would gladly enter more deeply into a parish community will be denied the opportunity. Without religious experience, the parish will have only "programs" and not the power of Baptism.

6. A Primary Task

Why doesn't the Church foster religious experiences? Possibly the example of Alcoholics Anonymous would help explain.

This organization has had a good degree of success — literally thousands owe their sobriety to A.A. The success results because A.A. sees helping alcoholics as its *primary task.*

The Catholic Church has the duty to help people experience God, but has never seen this task as *primary.* However, the "born-again Churches" see religious experiences as primary. They take the questions associated with religious experiences, and work out answers. Their success is seen in their growth.

The question remains, though, why does the Catholic Church not see fostering religious experiences as a primary concern? The Church shouldn't be faulted for not knowing everything about helping alcoholics. However, religious experiences flow from Baptism, and the Church is supposed to know everything possible about Baptism, for that is where it all begins for every Catholic.

1. The Match and The Candle

In the Charismatic Movement, the basic religious experience is called "The Baptism of the Spirit." meaning a Release of the sacrament's power within the person. Today about 8,000 are involved in this Movement in Philadelphia.

Two things should be noted:

1) 8,000 represents less than 1% of the Archdiocese.
2) The prayer groups are very fragile, and really do not have the resources to completely foster religious experiences.

The prayer groups are like a match which can light the candle of the Church. For only so long can the match remain lit. The permanency of the flame depends upon the candle receiving it.

Currently, the flame of religious experiences is fostered by a charismatic movement, but the movement will inevitably cease. The permanent question is, "Did the candle of the Church receive the light, or was the flame of Catholic Pentecostalism just one, brief, shining — but passing — moment of Church history?

23

The Gift
Of Community

That is why I kneel before the Father, from whom every family in heaven and on earth takes its name;.. (Eph 3:14)

They devoted themselves to the apostles instruction and the communal life, to the breaking of bread and the prayers. (Acts 2:42)

Much that the priest does is fairly easy. Most priests feel capable saying mass, hearing confessions or anointing the sick. Some normal priestly ministry is more difficult — preaching or teaching.

Two parts of priestly ministry are almost never done — the pastoral care involved in:

1) bringing about religious experiences.
2) forming Christian community.

It is the rare priest who seems to care about and have any skill in either of these tasks. Yet, both are the first fruits of Baptism.

We grow angry with someone who fathers a child and then walks away from the responsibilities involved. Likewise the Church cannot bring people to birth at Baptism and then walk away from two basic responsibilities — bestowing an experience of Jesus Christ and offering a Christian community.

Perhaps many baptized will never take advantage of that pastoral care, but at least it should not be the Church's fault that the Baptismal gifts are not fulfilled.

The following stories describe our present pastoral situation and encourage the priest to attempt to form Christian community.

1. What To Do During The Week

One time I was sitting next to my little first grade nephew as we watched his older brothers perform in *Brigadoon.* Unfortunately, they had told him the story. Toward the end of the show, he nudged me and asked "Are we in *Brigadoon,* Uncle Vince"? I didn't quite know what he meant. "You know, Uncle Vince," he continued, "are we in Brigadoon, so that when Brigadoon goes up, we go up with it?"

The basic pastoral problem for every priest is that on Sunday mornings, the parish, like Brigadoon, suddenly pops out of nowhere and then, after the last mass, seems to vanish until next Sunday.

Some priests would say "Well, that is the reality." We priests basically feel comfortable on Sunday morning. Out of nowhere converge all these people who quite docilely follow their leaflet missals and quite politely listen to our sermons and quite patiently await our "Go in peace, to love and serve the Lord." Then both priest and people seem happy that the weekly Brigadoon is successfully completed.

The real pastoral problem is to have Christian community exist every day. The parish community is not meant to disappear any more than the parish buildings.

Does the Father work only on Sundays? According to Jesus, He and the Father are always at work.

So a very real and truly devastating pastoral reality exists in practically every Catholic parish — no one, priest or people, seems to know what to do when mass is over to make the Christian community present.

2. "The Body"

Being deeply interested in religious experiences, I also became interested in Churches that built their entire life around these experiences. One day, driving through center city, I noticed a store-front Church.

The area's population was almost totally black, but inside this Church was a white man about thirty years old, reading a

Greek New Testament. His story shows the power of support in a close-knit Church community.

At 18, he had a religious experience, which he followed up with attendance at a denominational college. According to him, the theology courses didn't help. When he finished the college, he still had not found the conclusion to his religious experience. He then went for bible study after which he began this store-front Church.

He took me through the curtain to the heart of his Church. There was an assortment of chairs and benches, none of which matched, in a room holding 45 people. The Bible sat on a stand, and off to the right was a very old piano.

All during the conversation, he kept talking about "The Body," and the importance of "The Body." He mentioned a number of Church members who were off studying nursing, medicine, law etc., who get their emotional support from "The Body." By that term he meant the close-knit relationships brought about in this bible-believing Church planted in the heart of the ghetto. For some, it was the support they needed to get settled into a way of life.

He then mentioned a used clothing shop run by the Church. I took time to visit and was quite impressed by the obvious order and peace in the store, staffed by Church members. The two places were an oasis in the middle of a neighborhood racked by crime. The Church was a doorway to another world for anyone who cared to experience Jesus Christ.

The two features that marked this Church were the religious experience of the young man, and the power of a community that is willing to be put together into "The Body."

3. A Scattered Flock

The vigil of Pentecost, 1972, was also ordination day in Philadelphia. After experiencing the beauty of the ordination ceremony, I drove to a much smaller grouping. About 15 of us, who constituted the Merion prayer group, were coming together for our first full day of prayer.

The two events contained my whole life, my two worlds, —

the large world of the whole Church and the small world of those I prayed with.

In the car that day, there was a special feeling. If the day had ended with the ordination it would have been beautiful. Yet, after the ceremony everyone scattered. Here I was going to a group that was gathering, ready to spend the whole day seeking the Lord.

Gradually that little gathering grew, so that now we gather every vigil of Pentecost in a full Cathedral.

Every priest should have those two worlds. Certainly, a beauty exists as hundreds attend the Sunday liturgy. Yet after mass, the people scatter and for many priests that is their only world. They have no people who gather with them. No people who experience Jesus with them. The priest presides over a scattered flock.

Will the sheep always scatter so quickly to return only as a flock each Sunday? For many people that is the only commitment they know or are ready for. But others would willingly gather. They can be led to the beginning experience of Jesus Christ. Then both, priests and people can learn (by experience and mistakes) how to gather and not scatter.

If the priest never moves in that direction. If he puts aside religious experiences and their power to gather the sheep, then he is doomed to spend his priesthood saying "The mass is ended go in peace."

4. The Few And The Many

We began the Merion prayer group in September 1971. About a year later, the number attending was between fifteen and twenty. One Saturday evening as I was driving there, I began to have doubts. "What am I doing going over here for fifteen and twenty people every week?" Yet deep in my heart, I knew this group would grow. The doubt quickly passed because each time we came together, the Spirit was so obviously present. Sure enough, the group grew until it became so large the academy could no longer handle the numbers.

Numbers occupy a central thinking in a priest's mind. He instinctively thinks about the number of families in the parish and the number who come to mass. Being priests in the largest Church body in the United States, we have to be conscious of numbers. Besides all that, Catholicism by its very nature is a universal religion, embracing every personality type.

Concerning numbers, the priest needs wisdom. Jesus worked with the few and the many. The few were special and when the many walked away, He built His Church on the little band of apostles and disciples, who then took the message to the whole world.

5. Sharing A Common Experience

When a seminarian, involved in a prayer community was ordained, his reception was a particularly joyous one, for many from his community were young people. As I was leaving the hall, I saw a group of young people ahead who were also heading home. I caught up with them, looking forward to continuing the joyful reception. However, they were not members of the community, but relatives and neighborhood friends of the new priest. My experience with them was quite different. Their conversation was typically adolescent — all over the place about superficial hopes or passing concerns. The contrast in experiences was stark.

The young people who experienced a full Christian community had a common experience and common hopes. The other young people just shared the fragmentation the world has to offer.

6. Where Is The Christian Community?

This morning my parents drove me to the airport. During the ride I thought of God's gift of a close family life, and that he has allowed my parents to remain on earth for such a long time.

Over the weekend, two of the grandchildren had spent the days with Mom and Dad.

Just last night, I had enjoyed being with eighteen other priests for our monthly priest prayer-dinner.

Those three stories represent the spectrum of Christian community — the home, the extended family, the Church.

No single answer exists for anyone's life, but the person will have a lot better chance to find his personal answers if he shares in a Christian community, rather than being the lonely seeker.

Yet, where is the Christian community? A parish school gives it some reality. The Sunday mass bestows some more. But both of those are far from providing what is needed in today's world.

True Christian community, like everything else in the Church, is God's gift. But it will only be given fully if we seek.

24

Church Structure

"*I for my part declare to you, you are Rock, and on this rock I will build my Church. . . .*"

(Matt. 16:18)

"*I became a minister of this Church through the commission God gave me to preach among you his word in its fullness,*" (Col. 1:25)

In recent years, people have made tremendous demands upon the Church. Every problem and issue has been brought to the Church. The question always is, "What is the Church doing about poverty, or nuclear weapons, or illegal aliens, or gun control?

The Church has worked with these questions — to study, issue statements, and to change people's attitudes.

Now, however, another question is being posed — "What is the Church doing about religious experiences?

Most of the following stories do not have a "successful conclusion" but they present a new reality — confusion or leakage from the Church because people, for one reason or another, are not experiencing God there.

They also present a challenge of besides being a Church of God's sacraments to become a source of God experiences.

1. We Used To Be Catholics

At a Protestant Pentecostal meeting, I found myself standing next to two young people who said they would be getting married soon. Both were Catholics.

Their story was a common one — nominal practice (one had attended a Catholic High school) followed by a religious conversion, and then a "born-again" life in a Fundamental Church which understood that phenomena and had helped them receive a gift.

They were surprised that a priest understood anything about these experiences. I tried to tell them about seeking these experiences in the Catholic Church, but I knew the words were futile.

They had been in the Catholic Church and had never received any religious experiences there. Now that they had found the experiences outside the Church, they weren't going to go back.

And if they did return, what would they find? How many priests understand religious experiences and know how to help people with them?

2. A Born-Again Catholic

A high school chaplain told me about a girl who had been "born again." Unfortunately, this led her outside the Catholic Church. And even though the Church where she first had the experience is now gone, she joined another denomination.

The priest is reluctant to come down too hard on her because she described her life before the experience as all messed up in every way, and her life after the experience as one of prayer, bible reading, faithful church attendance.

The interesting part deals with the time when her first Church closed up. It would have been normal, at that time, for her to return to Catholicism. But, in spite of being just a high school student, and in spite of her Catholic background, she took the time to go to yet another denomination to find a Church that fostered her experiences (even though she was attending Catholic high school).

Most Catholics would ask, Why? Don't we have the highest form of worship in the Eucharist, and don't we have the bible and the liturgy of the word?" We do have all these things, but we don't place much emphasis on personal religious experiences. So when someone has these experiences and wants help, they don't find the Catholic Church that concerned. There are no structures for this type of pastoral help — so the people search out churches that do understand and foster what God is doing within.

3. What Sometimes Happens

In 1971, I met a married couple who were deeply prayerful, as well as committed to social justice, having opened their homes to refugee families.

Somewhere along the line, however, things went wrong and their religious experiences led them outside the Catholic Church. Not being directly associated with them, I don't know why, or what the particulars were.

The phenomenon, however, is growing across the country — not people dropping out of the Catholic Church because of lack of religious interest, but people dropping out because of intensity of religious interest.

Each case is different, and many factors enter into that decision. However, in many cases the cause is the lack of understanding of religious experiences by their local parish. These people use terms like, "I don't get fed there" or "I need a deeper fellowship."

I am not trying to justify leaving the Catholic Church as a valid result of religious experiences, but am pointing out that this "going elsewhere" is a growing phenomenon. In theory, the presence or lack of religious experiences shouldn't make any difference, since Catholic practice is rooted in doctrine and in truth. But we can't just feed people doctrine and truth.

It is sometimes difficult for lay people who understand and live religious experiences to relate to a Church where priests don't understand them. We priests are asking them to live in two different religious worlds, and that's difficult over a long period of time.

4. Where To Go?

Some people, after receiving the beginning religious gift, are so carried away with the discovery that they begin to criticize the Church, especially if this initiation has come through interdenominational sources. Their tendency, if not unchecked, is to take their experiences, get our their bible, and join what is called a "Bible-believing Church."

"Leaving the Church" isn't the usual result, especially if the beginning religious experience occurs within the Catholic Church. People can see the importance of Church structures, are grateful to the Church and find a new fervor for the Eucharist.

So, there is no need to "go elsewhere", but there is a growing need for the Church to provide fertile soil for the seed of religious experience to grow.

5. A House Full of Children

What will a wide-scale introduction and seeking of religious experiences do to the Catholic Church? Certainly many difficulties exist, but the same can be said of a houseful of children. At least that house has life, and growth, and a future.

Two important points should be noted:

1) The Church's theology provides a foundation for religious experiences and charisms.
2) The Church has handled these experiences for years — mainly in popular devotions and in religious communities.

There is too much theology and pastoral wisdom for the Catholic Church to be threatened by wide scale religious experiences.

The structure won't break. The walls won't come tumbling down. But we priests must be ready.

6. *Angry Prophets*

In the 1960's the Church had a lot of "prophets," people speaking out against "Church faults." They had a full catalogue of Church evils – a conservative pope, a stupid hierarchy, a Church absent from the ghetto, unaware of racial needs, insensitive to the pleas of priests and religious, aligned with the powerful friends of big business, immersed in politics, etc."

Various "name people" emerged in the criticism and became leaders who were followed by others who walked in their light. Various movements, formal and informal, emerged.

A lot of good people, priests, religious and lay, were involved in these movements that sought to change the Church. All too many are no longer with the Church – to nobody's credit.

What went wrong? Was it inevitable? Is someone always harmed or destroyed if they try to reform the Church? Without speaking against or about any given person, or idea, or reform, there does seem to be a lesson.

Changing the Church can only be safely undertaken by someone (or some group) who has already been deeply changed by religious experiences.

The powerful stream of true Church reform is always the stream of religious experiences. Only the powerful gift of the Spirit within the person can reform the Body of which that Spirit is the soul.

Most priests aren't called to reform the whole Church, but we are all called to reform the parish Church and to contribute to the reform of the local diocesan Church.

The beautiful phrase "Ecclesia semper reformanda est" has to do with every "ecclesia," and "semper" means every day. The burden rests with every priest, not just a few intellectuals. But there will be no stream of reform if there is no stream of religious experiences.

7. Why Do You Come?

In August 1971, a Mercy sister came to my office, saying that she felt called to start a prayer group for sisters and wanted me to be with her. So, we began — five of us, praying to receive the Lord's power. For the first two years, we were small, but then the growth came, until more than four hundred were meeting with us every week.

With the growth, I had to get to know the people. Each week I would gather twenty people asking them why they came. The stories were overwhelming — marriages restored, salvation from suicide, healings from alcoholism, return to the sacraments, finding a vocation. These were significant, life-changing results.

But I had to ask myself — why did they have to come to our prayer group to experience this? The answer always came back — because the average parish couldn't provide this. The average priest didn't understand God's power in a ministry based on religious experiences. But the day will come, when every parish will be the focus of these life-changing moments.

25

Conclusion

"Lord, to whom shall We Go."   *(Jn 6:68)*

". . . so if they tell you, 'Look, he is in the desert,' do not go out there; or 'He is in the innermost rooms,' do not believe it.' "   (Matt 24:26)

They went to the temple area together every day, while in their homes they broke bread . . . Day by day the Lord added to their numbers those who were being saved.   (Acts 2:46-47)

Today's reading at mass (Friday — Fifth Week of Lent) sums up this chapter,

> *Then he went back across the Jordan to the place where John had been baptizing earlier, and while he stayed there many people came to him. "John may never have performed a sign," they commented, "but whatever John said about this man was true."* (John 10:40-42)

The people in that gospel had a dream in their hearts. John was not the fulfillment of the dream, but was sent by God to point out Jesus.

This Jesus is so real, that we should meet Him, not only in our hearts, but in some external place. That place exists for every priest — the place where he will meet Jesus, and discover that everything I have said about Him "was true".

1. There Would Be Such A Place

As our Merion Prayer group continued to grow, we decided to do a slide presentation of our history. The week before we asked people to prepare a few words about what the prayer group meant to them. We didn't tell them that they would be recorded and photographed.

That night a twenty year old girl spoke the perfect words, almost straight out of Camelot:

> "In my heart I always believed there would be a
> place like Merion, and for years I searched. But
> when I walked in here I realized that what I had
> dreamed about, really existed."

When Jesus said, "Don't go to the upper room or don't go to the desert to find the Messiah", He didn't mean not to go anywhere. He meant for us not to believe in sensational rumors about extraordinary phenomena.

So if you dream of religious experiences; if you "always believed there would be a place like Merion", then look around you. The Lord has probably prepared a place where all described here is available to you.

2. He Lives

About 10 years ago, I saw the movie "Z" (He lives). It was a Greek film centering on a man who tried to help others to freedom from government repression. Toward the end, he is killed by these forces. However, his power didn't end with death, because the people he helped, carried him in their thoughts and in their minds, — "He lives".

Every author should ask what is unique about his book (otherwise why write?). The uniqueness about this book is that everything described here, lives.

A priest reader doesn't have to say, "that's nice theory." He doesn't even have to think, "I wish that could be for me." Everything described here lives in Philadelphia.

We have no buildings, no office, no budget, not even anyone "full time". But we have priests for whom Jesus Christ is alive. Our dream is that every priest would personally know this Jesus.

3. Seeking For Years

A year ago, a priest who left the active ministry in 1979, came to talk — not sure of what direction to take. A few months later he began coming to the priest prayer group. A month ago, he decided on a retreat so a firm decision could be made, one way or the other. Much has happened since then. By circumstances, he ended up speaking to the Cardinal about a return, two years to the day that he had asked for a leave.

During the retreat, as he began to experience God's closeness for the first time in his life. He said "For years, I went from priest to priest. All I wanted to do was to get to know Jesus Christ in a personal way, and nobody understood what I was asking for."

What he sought for years, he found — in a definite place in the Lord's time. For every priest who searches "to get to know Jesus Christ in a personal way," some place and time is set aside by God for the moment of the gift.

4. Philadelphia Will Do

In one of his movies, W. C. Fields was about to be lynched by an angry mob. He sought one last dying man's request, "I'd like to see Paris before I die." As the mob quickly vetoed that idea, he replied, "Well, Philadelphia will do."

If, as you look around, you cannot find a place where the living waters of a religious experience can be found, then maybe "Philadelphia will do." Any priest is welcome to come.

KEY OF DAVID BOOKS AND TAPES

The Power of David's Key is just one of the many books, tapes and videos written and produced by Monsignor Walsh. The following are some others which are available. The style is easy-to-read, the quality is excellent and the prices are always moderate.

To order: *Call/fax 610-896-1970*
Order on line: www.libertynet.org/~bvm

Key of David Publications
204 Haverford Road
Wynnewood, PA 19096

SCRIPTURE
***The Kingdom at Hand* (292 pages)**   *Price: $10.00*
A unique prayer book on St. Matthew's Gospel. The ideas are simple and clearly written. The reader experiences the power of the scriptural text itself.

THREE RECENT BOOKLETS
The Ten Commandments   *Price: $150 per 100*
                                    Individual copy: $6.00 ea.
This is the most extensive of the three booklets, providing a clear explanation of each commandment. Particularly helpful is the extensive wealth of the biblical texts which provide living examples of both good and sinful behavior.

What Catholics Believe (The Apostles Creed)   *Price: $50 per 100*
                                    Individual copy: $1.00 ea.
This booklet, actually written first, explains each phrase of the Apostles Creed, combining much modern scholarship with an easy to read style.

The Seven Sacraments   *Price: $100 per 100*
                                    Individual copy: 2.00 ea.
The booklet follows the same easy-to-read format of *What Catholics Believe,* explaining for each sacrament, the biblical foundation, the historical Church tradition, and the practical applications

BOOKS OF STORIES

The following three books have forty chapters each and are filled with stories:

Special Words Just For You   *Price: $5.00*
This book hopes to show everyone that God is active every day and in every type of circumstance. Hopefully, the reader's eyes will be opened to a fresh view of faith.

If God Wants a Steak, He Pays for a Steak   *Price: $5.00*
This book hopes to show everyone that the manifestations of the Spirit are happening in the Catholic Church and are available to any person who would seek and search for a full life in the Spirit.

To The Angel of the Church in Philadelphia   *Price: $4.00*
This book is a collection of thirty-two articles outlining the many beginning stories of the Spirit's work in Philadelphia.

SUNDAY HOMILIES
Sunday Homilies   *Price: $5.00*
Since 1996, the Sunday homilies have been recorded and are available (two per tape). Complete list available on our web site.

HISTORY OF EVANGELISM
What is Going On   *Price: $8.00*
Many Catholics are confused by the worldwide growth of Protestant Pentecostalism. In just 189 pages, Monsignor Walsh provides a clear view of the history and dynamism behind Protestant Evangelism.

CHARISMATIC RENEWAL
These books provide a strong foundation, both in Charismatic spirituality and Church teaching:

A Key to Charismatic Renewal in the Catholic Church   (286 pages)
                                        Price: $6.00
The book is known for its clear description of the Charismatic Movement and has become a worldwide classic (also in Spanish).

Lead My People   Price: $4.00
This is a manual for those who guide a prayer group, large or small. The manual is also helpful to everyone who participates in a weekly prayer meeting.

Prepare My People   Price: $5.00
This book contains eight chapters on the beginning Pentecostal experiences and chapters on spiritual growth after receiving these initial gifts.

Teach My People   Price: $4.00
This book is a companion volume to *Lead My People*. Its purpose is to help leaders with the charism of teaching. It provides solid material for Catholic teachings.

Keep the Flame Alive   Price: $5.00
The first eight chapters explain Catholic teaching so that Catholics appreciate the traditions of their 2000-year historical Church. The second section is a dictionary of Charismatic terminology. The third part is a teaching on prayer tongues which shows how this gift matures and leads into other charisms.

VIDEOCASSETTES
Revival Fires in the Catholic Church   Price: $25.00
The Living Waters of Charismatic Revival   Price: $15.00

Please call or fax for <u>free</u> materials and a complete catalog. Discounts are available to any group that will sell the materials.

AUDIOTAPES
The Spirit and the Church   Price: $60.00
(20 part – 15 cassette Series on Catholic Pentecostalism)
These tapes have the same scope of purpose as *A Key to Charismatic Renewal* – a full teaching on the basic powers of the Renewal. The tapes are filled with person stories and examples. These cassettes were professionally recorded and duplicated. The talks are teachings that offer a definite vision and wisdom on the Renewal.

Revival in the Catholic Church   Price: $10.00
The clearest and most extensive teaching on Revival and its history at Presentation B.V.M. Parish.

NOTES